THE HYNES OF IRELAND

by

James Patrick Hynes

Front Cover: 'Dunguaire Castle', a painting by the author

As the former Mayor of County Galway (2005 – 2006) and as a Citizen of the County of Galway bearing the surname of one of the greatest and oldest Gaelic families of Connaught, I am pleased to recommend this excellent book by James Patrick Hynes who has been the first to record and present a history of King Guaire, "The Generous", sixth century King of Connaught and his descendants.

The people and events mentioned here may have been forgotten during recent times but through the scholarly efforts of my kinsman James P Hynes, their memories have now been restored to their rightful place in the history of Ireland.

COUNCILLOR PAT HYNES

(Member of Galway County Council & Loughrea Town Council)

The Author

James Patrick Hynes, M.A., was born in 1930 in Liverpool where his secondary education was undertaken first at St. Elizabeth's Central School and then at St. Edward's College. After National Service with British Army on the Rhine he worked in insurance, shipping and fire fighting before following a career as a teacher in Britain and Canada and lecturing in English and in Education in his city of birth.

He has qualifications from the Universities of London, Hull, Victoria in Canada and the University of Liverpool.

Over many years he has contributed articles to newspapers and magazines and has written various short local history guide books on places in Ireland and Wales.

He is the author of various books including *The O'Shaughnessys* , *Lawrence of Arabia's Secret Air Force: based on the diary of Flight Sergeant George Hynes* published by Pen and Sword. Flight Sergeant George Hynes was the author's uncle

Contents

"THE LAND OF GLORIOUS AIDHNE"

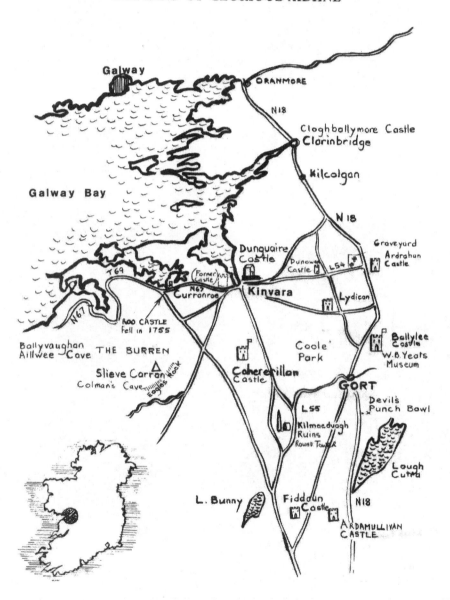

Foreword

Dunguaire Castle stands on the rocky shoreline of an inlet called Kinvara Bay, part of the larger and world-famous Galway Bay on the west coast of Ireland. Owen O'Heyne, Lord of Aidhne built the present castle in the early Sixteenth Century on the site of the Seventh Century palace of his ancestor, King Guaire, the Hospitable, King of Connaught.

Much of this book concerns the life and legends of King Guaire mac Colmain, who lived in the ancient palace of Raith Durlais until his death in the year 663. The poets of old knew his ancient ringfort on the shore of Kinvara Bay as:

> *The white sheeted fort of soft stones*
> *Habitation of poets and bishops*

The rest of the book is about the descendants of Guaire: particularly the O'Hynes and the O'Shaughnessys and to a lesser extent the other lineal descendants of that Seventh Century king - the O'Clearys, the O'Cahans, the O'Cahills and the Killikellys (Kilkellys). Their ancient friends and foes are mentioned too: among them - the Berminghams, Burkes, De Lacys, Fitzgeralds, Gregorys, Martins, MacDermots, MacFirbis's, MacNamaras, O'Briens, O'Connors, O'Donnells, O'Dowds, O' Flahertys, O'Kellys, O'Loughlins, O'Moghans and the O'Neills and others whose names and deeds have been mentioned in the history of the territory of the Ui Fiahrach Aidhne over the past 2000 years or so.

This history should be of interest not only to the numerous descendants of King Guaire but also to the many visitors who call at the Castle of Dunguaire each year and to those who visit the Aillwee Cave, the W.B. Yeats Museum at Ballylee, the Burren, Clontarf, Clonmacnoise, Galway, Gort, Innis Cealtra, Kilmacduagh, Lough Cutra and Raftery's Grave in Ireland.

A few lines about Dunguaire Castle inspired my first history of Guaire and his descendants from the Shell Book of Ireland back in 1980. That reference to Dunguaire led to visits to the libraries of the Universities of Liverpool and Manchester; to libraries in Dublin and Galway and to on-site visits to many of the places mentioned here. That book, the first ever history of the Hynes and O'Shaughnessys, was then reproduced on a tabletop lithographic printer. Now much of the information given here can be found on the Internet. Interested readers may now fruitfully follow up various references without leaving their chairs at home.

Non-Irish speakers will find it difficult to recognise and pronounce many of the names given here. Occasionally the English equivalent has been given but readers should acknowledge the Irish rendering and patiently read on.

Early Ireland

Dungaire Castle, Kinvara, in County Galway, on the west coast of Ireland, sits on a coastal promontory bridging thirteen centuries of history by linking the Seventh Century King Guaire (pronounced 'Goora') with his twenty first century descendants. The Castle, a prominent landmark at the head of the waters of Galway Bay, is owned and managed by the Shannon Development Company who have opened this O'Hynes tower house to the public. Twice an evening for five months of the year, paying guests take part in medieval banquets on the site from which, thirteen hundred years ago, the King of Connaught's Easter Feast was miraculously transported to his hermit cousin some five miles away. Near this very spot, King Guaire Aidhne's (Hynes) famous palace once lay.

Guaire's 'palace', probably a large hill fort, Dun Guaire, and his other palace at Gort, some six miles away to the south-east, lay in the territory of the tribe of the Ui Fiachrach Aidhne (pronounced 'O'Feery Hyne') and Guaire was their most generous ruler and most famous King of Connaught.

Like so many of the ancient Irish kings, Guaire could ingeniously and inventively trace his ancestry back to Adam and Eve and although that process of genealogical perfection has been lost, his progenitors have been traced back to Eochy Muigh (Yohee Mew) or Moyvane who ruled Connaught between AD 358 and AD 365, father of the celebrated Niall of the Nine Hostages. Eochy, who was known as the 'Lord of the Slaves', is said to have had three sons from whom descended the 'Connachta', and another son Niall, from whom descended the Ui Neill, Kings of Ireland, and traditional enemies of the Connachta. These Connachta sons were called - Fiachra, Brion and Ailella - so their descendants were correspondingly: the Ui Fiachrach, the Ui Briuin and the Ui Ailella. The Ui Fiachrach were divided as the Ui Fiachrach of the north (among whom the O'Dowds were prominent) and the Ui Fiachrach of the south, the Ui Fiachrach Aidhne, who supplied at least five Kings of Connaught.

Prince Fiachra commanded the army of Niall when he defeated the Munster forces from whom he exacted the Nine Hostages, who through their treachery eventually brought about his death, having him buried alive in

Moy Goish in Westmeath. Fiachra, of 'the Flowing Hair', had five sons, the most famous of whom was Dathy, so called because he could arm himself very quickly, an ancestor of the O'Heynes, O'Clearys, O'Shaughnessys, Kilkellys and others. Dathy was styled King of Ireland, of Alba (Scotland) and of 'Brittain'. After 150 successful battles he conquered territories as far as the Alps where he "was killed by lightning" as he attacked a fortress in those mountains. One wonders why he was fighting such a long way from home! It is said however that the tribes of the Ui Fiachrach Aidhne were descended from the Concani of Spain, a brave martial race descended from the Scythians so perhaps it should be no surprise to learn that King Dathy knew his way to the Danube!

This man, Dathy, last pagan King of Ireland, ancestor of the tribes of the Ui Fiachrach Aidhne, had many sons, one of whom, Ollioll Molt (d. 484) succeeded as King of Connaught and as monarch of Ireland. His third son, Eochaid Breac had a son, Eoghan (Owen), who became known as Eoghan Aidhne as he had been fostered by the Firbolg tribe which lived in the territory of Aidhne. (Fostering was an ancient system whereby children were given over to the chieftains of other tribes to be brought up as their own. This was a way of forging strong familial alliances.) The title Aidhne continued down the centuries becoming Ui Aidhne, Ui hEidhne, O Heyne and in its most recent anglicised form, Hynes. Eoghan Aidhne had four sons Conall, Cormac, Seuona and Seachnasach, progenitors of the principal tribes.

How can we be reasonably sure of the historical truth of this genealogy? Was it all oral tradition or was some of it recorded in 4th. and 5th.century ogham script on permanent rocks then later in Latin after St.Patrick's endeavours much of which could have been destroyed during Viking raids on monasteries? Perhaps it was all of those sources and then taken up in the medieval Irish uncial script reflecting the Irish version of a language used by other Q-Celtic speakers sharing root words and phrases with them. No doubt too sharing ancient stories and folk memories of a common ancestry with the P-Celtic speakers in Wales, Cornwall and Brittany. The stories are as reliable as any other pre-historic source.

The earliest human settlements in Ireland began about 7000 years ago during the Early Bronze Age. Evidence of early ongoing cultivation is best illustrated by field systems found under the blanket bogs in Ceide Fields in northwest Mayo. The many megalithic court, portal and passage tombs found throughout the land are also tangible evidence of early communities about whom we know so little. Their stone works were impressive as tangibly witnessed by Irish passage graves especially the one at Newgrange, constructed about 1,000 years earlier than the third phase of Stonehenge. Only very recently has it been concluded that during the morning of the winter solstice the Sun's rays shone through a special aperture as a beam of light gradually creeping along a 19 metre long passageway to bathe the central burial chamber in morning light.

Early Ireland was divided into a number of petty kingdoms or 'tuatha' about 150 of them. (Tuatha was a collective term denoting a group of persons who bore a common surname and lived independently, under their own kings.) Several tuatha would voluntarily join together to form larger kingdoms. One such kingdom was Connaught, and there, King Guaire in his time, the mid seventh century, ruled one fifth of Ireland. The other fifths were Ulster, Munster, Meath and Leinster frequently at war with each other like other regions inhabited by war loving human beings! The Ui Fiachrach Aidhne territory where Guaire ruled, lay in Western Ireland, in what is now known as County Galway. Today's place name, Clarina, in County Limerick, is a derivative of Clar Aidhne, The Great Meadow of the Aidhne, possible the southernmost point of the Aidhne territory stretching northwards to Oranmore westwards Galway Bay and eastwards to the Slieve Aughty Mountains. However at the height of their power in the seventh century, the Ui Fiachrach Aidhne had all the territory southwards to the Shannon, a natural barrier, but even so Guaire's influence was felt in Limerick and its surrounding countryside.

The lands west of the Shannon were places where the brothers of Niall of the Nine Hostages had set up their dynastic lines. Much further north, the Ui Fiachrach Muaide ruled in the Moy estuary which was rich in salmon and fertile land. The Fir Chera ruled in Carra, Mayo, while the Ui Fiachrach Aidhne's territory ended hard up against Munster in the southern reaches of Connaught. Although each of the Ui Fiachrach had supplied kings of Connaught for many centuries, eventually the Ui Briuin came to monopolise that position

The inhabitants of pre-Christian Ireland, before Guaire's time were thought to be the natural descendants of Celts from Europe, probably from North Western France and the Rhineland and these peoples supplanted or absorbed the original inhabitants of Ireland who had lived there long ago. Those original peoples were expert in mining and metalwork and their skills were adopted by the invading Celts. Mythical earlier peoples were said to have been driven off the land surfaces to live below the ground becoming the fairyfolk of legend.

These peoples of ancient Ireland developed a hierarchical tribal system with four or five status levels: the upper class (the rulers and warrior kings); the professional class (the administrators); the free (who could own cattle and become warriors); and the unfree, the slaves. The aristocracy, the 'airl aicme', surrounded and supported the king and their property, principally cattle, was defined and protected by Brehon law. Separate individual families were the real units of society but they acted corporately and were responsible for the observance of the law based on an individual's identity, clan and personal wealth.

A rural economy was the basis for a sophisticated system of law concerned in minutest detail with the management of land and animals and with the everyday business of milling, malting, meat preparation, spinning and weaving. The rulers and their professional advisers spent most of their time in the maintenance of law and order, hence, wisdom in administration was expected of them. Eloquence and skill at arms were much prized qualities expected and exercised by chieftains. Women were accorded parity with men, at least among the aristocracy, and, even well into the Christian era women often fought alongside men in some of the battles. The activities of Maeve, an early Queen of Connaught, are quite revealing in this respect.

The economic bases of society were cattle raising and raiding and an agriculture in which the principal crops were wheat, barley, oats, flax and hay. Sheep were bred for their wool used in the manufacture of clothing. Large woollen cloaks, fastened with ornamental brooches at the shoulder, were the most widely used outer garments, worn over tunics made of linen, tied at the waist by belts or girdles. The upper classes wore shoes of leather and their bodies were adorned with beautifully wrought ornaments of gold. The Tara Brooch kept in the National Museum of Ireland is the most well known ornamental object from the eighth century exemplifies the best in Irish craftsmanship at a time when the people were the most cultured in Europe. Irish silver and gold work has been described as, 'the work of angels'. In earlier times clothing could have included flowing kilts. Warriors would have been armed with swords and spears and protected by helmets and shields, all wonderfully ornamented. Judging from the evidence showing up in the ornamentation of weapons of war from all over the globe, there seems to be an innate universal desire for humans to decorate their killing tools! The Irish certainly did as did other peoples.

The Irish were scrupulously clean using soap in their ablutions and regularly wearing perfume. Cooking and drinking vessels included vats and iron urns, goblets and mugs. Dwellings for the most part were made of wattle and daub situated when possible on natural or artificial islands on lakes. An excellent example of such a lake dwelling may be seen at the Craggaunowen Project near Quin in County Clare. There the late Mr. John Hunt restored a medieval castle and began the construction of a crannog or lake dwelling. Crannogs were artificial islands constructed in rivers, lakes and waterways using oak piles and beams, wattle and daub and thatch and very comfortable and roomy homes they were. Some 2000 such can still be found in Ireland.

The land of Ireland itself was a mass of carboniferous limestone, nowhere more obvious than in the County of Galway today. This land was badly drained as impervious boulder clay prevented the rains from penetrating the surface. Bogs abounded; the most famous of them the Bog of Allen lay in the middle of the island stretching over some twenty miles. Roads criss-crossed the central lowland along sandy ridges which are in

A Crannog

fact the eskers or sediment from the streams which flowed beneath the ice sheet that once covered the land long ago. Around the coast were many coastal loughs and narrow inlets and again the most beautiful of them are to be found on the west coast. Guaire's palace and the subsequent

O'Hynes Castle sat at the head of one such inlet, that of Kinvara Bay and another O'Hynes Castle once stood at the head of Corran Roo Bay just four miles west of Dungaire but it fell during the earthquake of faraway Lisbon in 1755.

Ireland has geological and ethnic ties with Wales, Scotland and Cornwall. In fact it is said that at one time King Guaire sought refuge with the Welsh during his conflict with Diarmid, the High King of Ireland. It was of course through Ireland's links with Wales that Christianity came to Eire. Even before St. Patrick's dramatic conversions, Christianity had crept into Ireland from Britain: possibly carried there by slaves made captive by Irish raiders. In the year 493 AD and a century or two later, during the reign of King Guaire, Christianity had been well established and Ireland was making a name for itself as the spiritual and scholastic centre of Europe while Guaire's reputation for generosity was being built upon his patronage of the holy men of Connaught and Munster. Visitors to Kilmacduagh today may see the ruins of the ecclesiastical buildings on sites begun in the seventh century in meadows given to St. Colman by King Guaire, the Generous. The nearby holy wells are dedicated to Saint Colman. For example, Tobermacduagh or the Well of Duach's Son, lies about a quarter of a mile from Kinvarra wrote Dr. Petrie in the 'Dublin Penny Journal' of 1832.

Guaire Becomes King of Connaught

The territory of the Ui Fiachrach Aidhne was important long before the days of King Dathy, claimed by many an Irish tribe as their forbear. It was said that Queen Maeve who undertook the Cattle Raid of Cooley, ruled there and there too, 'In the 'year of the world', A.M. 3727, Magh Aidhne, the Plain of Aidhne, was the scene of many battles involving the monarch Muirceamhan. He was the first to insist upon chiefs wearing chains of gold around their necks as a mark of nobility. Fin MacCumhail (Fin MacCool), the mythical hunter-warrior, defeated the chieftain Uinche in battle at Ceann Mara, today's seaside town of Kinvara. Uinche managed to escape and to demolish Fin's palace but Fin pursued him and slew him at Uinche's Ford in Kilmacduagh. It was here too that the lovers, Diarmid and Graine were pursued by Fin through the woods of Doire Dhe Bhoth, later known as Chevy's Chase, a valley lying between Lough Cutra and Loughgraney in the O'Hynes /O'Shaughnessy lands. The Lady Echtge, one of the Tuatha De Danaan (the fairy kind) gave her name to the mountains bordering O'Shaughnessy land. The hills are now known as the Sliabh Eachta, Slieve Aughty.

For centuries, both before and after the reign of Guaire Aidhne, the kingship of Connaught was held in turn by the Ui Fiachrach of the north, the Ui Fiachrach of the south, the Aidhne and the Ui Briuin, according to which dynasty had the strongest candidate at the time; usually the one with the best skill at arms! Such candidates had to have the power to gain the kingship and to hold it in spite of the exacting demands made upon the holder. Early attempts by the Ui Niall to seize power in Connaught met with little success as in 538 AD when Diarmid Mac Corbaill's brother, Maine (not Ui Maine,) was slain in battle at Claenloch near Gort while trying to claim Ui Maine (O' Kelly) lands. The Annals of Tigernach say he was killed by an ancestor of Guaire's, Goibhneann mac Conaill. Determined attempts by the Ui Niall to gain Ui Maine failed, and those lands became part of Connaught. It was incumbent upon chieftains not only to defend his own territory, people and possessions, but to wrest as much as he could from other tribes and territories. Human nature across time and cultures seem to exercise that principle universally and those 'practising' Christianity were never any different and sometimes worse! Christianity although preaching peace had little influence on the morality of princes and kingdoms constantly waging war. Today is no different in this respect except that in earlier millennia most killing was 'up close and personal' whereas today mass slaughter can be carried out from great distances with very expensive technology.

Traditionally, Christianity entered Ireland with St.Patrick who died in AD 461 on March 17 so by the time Guaire's grandparents struggled in their kingships the fundamental tenets of that religion had taken hold in Connaught.

531 AD

In 531 AD, Goibhneann, chief of the Ui Fiachrach Aidhne, became King of Connaught after defeating the King of Ui Maine at the battle of Claenloch in Cinel Aidhne (possibly on Clar Aidhne which is now Clarina near Limerick). It is possible that Goibhneann was the great grandfather of Guaire while on the other hand he could have been the brother of Guaire's grandfather who was called Gubran.

622 AD 627 AD

The first of the Ui Fiachrach Aidhne, to become King of Connaught, was the chieftain Colman mac Cobthaig who became the eleventh king of the province. He lost the kingship after being killed by Rogallach mac Uatach of the Ui Briuin at the battle of Cenn Bugo (Cambo) in Roscommon in the year 622 AD. It is quite likely that Guaire's father, this Colman, had been an able king for his reign seems to have passed quietly enough before his death. Guaire's career began about this time when, he, a young prince of the Aidhne, was defeated just a few years later in battle in the year 627 during what is thought to have been an attempt to recapture territory to the south of the Slieve Aughty Mountains from the King of Cashel. Some sources suggest that the battle was actually against the Munstermen who had invaded the Ui Fiachrach lands. This humiliation of Guaire in battle, occurred at Cam Fearadhaigh or Cahernarry in Limerick and with him, in retreat, went Conall of the northern branch while among the dead princes were Conall, chief of the Ui Maine (think of O'Kelly), Maeldubh, Maelduin, Maelruain, Maelreasil and Meahealgaigh. The place where they fell was thereafter called 'the ford of the slaughtering of the six'. Guaire must have been very young on that occasion but at least he survived long enough to find immortality in the annals of Irish history and poetry.

In his turn, Rogallach, who died in 649 was possibly the first of the Ui Briuin to hold the provincial kingship after ousting Colman mac Cobthaig. Following the Battle of Cahernarry, the Ui Fiachrach Aidhne must have been somewhat weakened as it left Rogallach mac Uatach in undisputed possession of the Kingship of Connaught. Nevertheless his triumph was short-lived, for, several years later Rogallach himself was killed. Some say he met an ignominious death in a brawl over the ownership of an animal killed in a hunt and that he was hacked to death by peasants' spades. It is more likely, however, that he was killed in battle by Mael Brigte mac Moth Iachan in the Ui Briuin's home territory.

Colman's sons, Guaire Aidhne mac Colman, d.633 and Laidgnen (Loingsech mac Colmain), in turn became Kings of Connaught after Rogallach's reign. After Rogallach's death, Guaire's brother ruled as King of Connaught, so Laidgnen or Loinsech of Aidhne was the thirteenth king of that territory until his death in 655 AD. It is possible that Laidgnen's widow, Deog, daughter of the King of Cashel later married her brother-in-law, Guaire, yet, on the other hand, Guaire is said to have been married to Ornait, daughter of Cuan, a later King of Cashel. It is possible, of course, that he married the one after the other or indeed at the same time, such was the practice of Irish kings, Christians or not!

These battles and killings among rival clans to gain ascendency and territory are practised by a majority of peoples, all through time, all through place and all over the world. During recent centuries, such murderous rivalry may have disappeared in Ireland and much of Europe but they have persisted in countries like Iraq where the most militaristically competent invader, the USA, has no idea how to subdue a country filled with pre-medieval rival clans still determined to continue tribal clashes!

Guaire became the fourteenth King of Connaught, probably in 655 AD and his reign is said to correspond with the peak of Ui Fiachrach power. Many stories are told of his legendary hospitality and indeed he became the Irish poets' epitome of the virtue of generosity. In fact it is held that his right arm was longer than his left as a result of his lavish donations of charitable gold!

THE DEATH OF SAINT CELLACH

Some stories told of Guaire seem to run counter to his virtuous nature by representing him in an uncomplimentary light. For example, his very accession to the kingship is associated with an alleged conspiracy in the death of a St. Cellach (Kelly) who had a claim to the kingship. In Guaire's day, the Ui Fiachrach territories, certainly those of the northern branch, extended north to the River Moy which was rich in fish and it included Killala Bay in today's County Sligo. There, the present suburb of Ballina, called Ardnarea, is linked with an uncharacteristic piece of treachery instigated by King Guaire. The precise location of the misdeed is said to appear in a history of the Ui Fiachrach written by MacFirbis who was recounting the deeds of the northern branch notably the O'Dowds.

Of course it should be borne in mind that within the 'historical' records of the seventh century, history and the legends are so inextricably woven together that it is well nigh impossible to separate the two, and to distinguish one from the other. Fact and fiction, truth and legend intermingle with each other. Sometimes truth contradicted legend and at other times legend complements truth.

Although Guaire was a powerful and indeed popular monarch, rivals claimed that he was not the true heir to the throne because Cellach (Kelly), son of a former king, Owen Bel, fourth in succession to Dathy had a better claim to the succession. Cellach had given up his life as a warrior to enter the priesthood, eventually becoming the Bishop of Kilmore-Moy but he was prevailed upon to leave his priestly life and to take up the kingship. He never made it. Guaire was said to have persuaded four ecclesiastical students, his own foster brothers in tutelage to him, to kill the rival, St. Cellach.

In this particular version of the story, the four Maels, so-called because each of their names began with that syllable (as did the four Maels mentioned above in the battle of Cam Fearadhaigh) Mael Da Lua, Mael Shenaigh, Mael Deoraidh and Mael Chroin waylaid Cellach and murdered him on the road. Shortly after the murder, Cellach's brother hunted down the murderers and brought them in chains to Castle Hill, near Ballina then called Tullanafarkshina, the hill of the prospect of the Moy. There, the killers were hanged and ever afterwards the hill was called Ard-na-riaghadh (Ardnarea) or the hill of execution. The bodies were interred on the other side of the river, south of today's Ballina, in the hill of the four Maels, Ard-na-Mael. A dolmen, dating from about 2,000 B.C., is a marker for the burial place. The dolmen was called the Table of Giants, because seventh century Irish believed such standing stones to be, indeed, the work of giants who lived there in ancient times.

Other versions of this tale agree in principle but vary in time and place. According to Sigerson's translation in 'Bards of Gael and Gaul', Eogan (Owen) Bel, King of Connaught and father of Cellach, plundered every province in the land. The people of Munster and Leinster paid him homage and taxes but Ulster resisted fiercely. At last the two kings of Ulster, Fergus and Domnall gathered a large army and attacked Connaught plundering the land as far as the Moy. Then at Sligo, Eogan Bel defeated them using only one battalion of his against five battalions of Ulster men. In that battle, both Ulster kings were slain outright but Eogan Bel was grievously wounded and had to be carried from the field of battle. His dying wish was for his son Cellach to be made king since Muiredach his youngest was still too young for the kingship. Ingeniously the Connaught chieftains buried Eogan standing upright, spear in hand, facing Ulster where even in death he would keep them out of Connaught! So great was the Ulstermen's fear of the dead hero that they eventually dug him up and buried him face downwards near Loch Gill.

These chieftains then had a problem on their hands for Cellach had become a monk in Clonmacnoise and his superior, St. Ciaran, would not release the young man from his vows to return to the life of a warrior. Poor Cellach, under pressure from his warrior friends, left the monastery without his abbot's permission and consequently St. Ciaran cursed him saying he would die a violent death for his disobedience. Guaire, it is said, was to be the instrument of that death.

Cellach, as king of the northern Ui Fiachrach and Guaire, as king of the southern Fiachrach, frequently disputed the boundaries of their territories so that one day, Guaire invited Cellach to a meeting but treacherously attacked him there, killing his friends and forcing Cellach to flee. Then for over a year, the bereft Cellach wandered the wilderness filled with anguish for having abandoned his monastery. At last, he repented and returned to Clonmacnoise and to his priestly duties, growing in holiness and learning so that at last he was elected Bishop of Killala.

There then came a time when Bishop Cellach visited his flock near Rath Durlas, possibly the promontory fort near Dunguaire Castle but more than likely another Dun Guaire, near Killala , County Mayo variously known as Durlussium, Raith Durlais ('strong fort') and Durlus Muaide because it is in the territory of the Ui Fiachrach Muaide. King Guaire summoned him to his palace, but, since it was noon on Saturday when Guaire's message arrived, Cellach refused to violate the Sabbath by travelling. Instead, said Cellach, King Guaire must visit the bishop on Sunday to hear mass or alternatively the bishop would visit Guaire on the Monday. An angry Guaire ordered Cellach out of his kingdom immediately before his church was burned over his head.

In the course of time, St. Cellach retired to live as a hermit on a lake island as so many had done before him. There, he lived with four companions; Mael Da Lua, Mael Shenaigh, Mael Deoraidh and Mael Chroin. Cellach's younger brother, who had become king of the northern Ui Fiachrach, regularly sought advice from his older brother during visits to the island  hermitage but Guaire took these visits to be plots hatched against him. Consequently, it is said, Guaire invited Cellach to a feast at which he was supposed to be poisoned but Cellach would not leave his island to attend. At Guaire's invitation though, the four Maels met the king and after promises of land and wives agreed to murder Cellach. After seizing the saint, they took him to the mainland, to a forest to murder him.

The Death of Saint Cellach

The saint, guessing the evil intentions in the hearts, begged them to reconsider so the murderers kept him imprisoned in a hollow tree overnight while they slept. Cellach, filled with great terror at his imminent death could not sleep but after many hours of soul searching he became reconciled to his death as the will of God so that by morning when he died he was quite calm. His body was left in the forest but the ravens and wolves which ate of his body became ill and died!

GUAIRE'S PALACE IS CURSED!

On reporting to Guaire, the four students were rewarded with wives and land. Meanwhile Muiredach searched the woodlands and discovered the remains of his brother's body taking it for burial on a bier pulled by tame deer which stayed near the grave to tend it ever afterwards. Muiredach, (Murdoch) also known as Cu Choingelt, and his followers, swore vengeance on the murderers and after a short stay with the chief of Ui Maine they travelled to Tara where they stayed with Blathmac, the king of all Ireland. Before long Blathmac's daughter, Aife fell in love with the handsome Muiredach and after marrying him she persuaded him to continue his search for the killers to avenge his brother's death.

Eventually, Muiredach, while out hunting, met a swineherd who warned him that he was trespassing on the land of the Four Maels. The swineherd was persuaded to lead Muiredach to the house of the Maels who were feasting and drinking whereupon Muiredach and his friends fell upon them, cutting their limbs from their bodies while they were still alive and hanging their bodies on sharp stakes to die slowly. According to this tale the execution place was called Ard na Raig or the hill of the gibbets.

Soon afterwards Muiredach became lord of the northern Ui Fiachrach and of Tirawley while Guaire ruled the southern Ui Fiachrach Aidhne. Fierce battles took place between them until Geilgeis, daughter of Guaire married Muiredach and the marriage brought temporary peace between the kingdoms. In the course of time, however, Muiredach began plundering in Guaire's lands so Guaire asked St. Ciaran to persuade Muiredach to visit Aidhne to make peace. Despite a premonition, a dream in which Muiredach felt, 'the swine of the son of Colman rending me', he travelled to Durlas in Kinvara where he was entertained for three days and three nights and

an alliance was agreed between the two kings in Ciaran's presence but…
as soon as Ciaran left, Guaire slew Muiredach and that was certainly not a
generous act!

The poem which recounts this story goes on to say how St. Ciaran cursed
Guaire for his treachery and that the cursing led to the fall of Guaire's Palace
of Durlas. The cursing is the poetic 'explanation' for the abandonment of
the hill fort at Kinvara until the erection of the O'Hynes Castle close by
in the sixteenth century.

Guaire's supposed relationship with St. Cellach has been likened to Henry
II's relationship with St. Thomas a Becket but most of the evidence
suggests that the story is no more than poetic fancy. The picture of Guaire
as a scheming villain is in its way a backhanded compliment by the poets
as the king is accorded sufficient status to be the subject of a romantic
tale. However R.J. Kelly has given the story in his article submitted to the
Royal Society of Antiquaries of Ireland in 1914. Kelly cites the Book of
the Hy Fiachrach as his source but the very date given for the battle in
which Cellach's father was killed gives us a clue to the improbability of the
story as fact as the date given was 537 AD! Even if Guaire had been born
that year he would have been ninety years old during the battle against
Failbe Flann and one hundred and twenty-six when he died! However,
Kelly's suggestion that St.Cellach has given his name to Disert Kelly in the
diocese of Kilmacduagh, traditional O'Hynes territory, is an interesting
observation for Disert means a lonely secluded spot and the place where
Cellach met his death. The site lies in a wood between Lough Conn and
Lough Ciullin in the Parish of Tirawley.There may well have been a Cellach
who died in unfortunate circumstances as described by the poets but not
the Cellach, son of Eogan Bel who was killed in either 543 AD or in 547
AD.

King Guaire and the Fall of Tara

The story of the cursing of Guaire by Saint Ciaran is only one of the many legends in which Guaire is the leading figure. He appears as the central character in another cursing, that of the High King of Ireland by Saint Ruadan. As Saint Ciaran's curse is said to have led to the downfall of the palace at Kinvara and the fall of the 'house' of Aidhne, so, Saint Ruadan's curse led to the fall of Tara, the legendary seat of power of the high kings of Ireland. This tale too puts Guaire in a bad light on the one.hand while on the other hand it suggests that Guaire displayed heroic qualities in his resistance to the attempted domination of Connaught by the Ui Neills, the High Kings. The fall of Tara symbolizes the Celtic inability to unite nationally under one powerful king. Such disunity among Celtic chieftains in Ireland, Scotland and Wales led to their eventual conquest by the English in the course of time.

According to this legend, King Diarmid mac Áedo Sláine, attempted to curb the power of the other Irish chieftains by getting them to pull down their fortifications, usually earth ramparts, or to modify them, to weaken them, so that they would offer less resistance to his own warriors. The High King's attempts were bitterly resisted by the chieftains although the High King's resolutions had been backed by the "parliament' at Tara. But "There was at the time, in Connaught, a king who held many smaller kings there under his authority. He was a very good king in his way and the most generous and munificent Irish king of whom there is any record, and the most hospitable man who ever appeared in Ireland. His name was Guaire" (Ireland: Her Story by S. O'Grady).

When the High King's officer approached Guaire's Castle to ask him to pull down his ramparts so that the High King's spear might pass through them, Guaire was so angry that he slew the messenger! This act of defiance was too much for King Diarmid so he gathered a large army drawn from the tribes of the lesser kings who had accepted his authority without resistance, among them men of Connaught, who were jealous of Guaire. After crossing the Shannon, the High King and his host attacked Guaire who was defeated in the ensuing battle and was forced to seek refuge. Guaire went into exile while lesser kings took fright at the High King's wrath and hastily pulled down their fortifications lest the anger of Tara should fall upon them.

In his turn, Diarmid was afraid that the outlawed Guaire would lead a strong resistance against him so he decided to capture him. Meanwhile, Guaire had sought and obtained sanctuary in Munster with a holy man, one of the renowned band of hermits whom Guaire had constantly helped. This holy man , fearing that the High King would break sanctuary persuaded Guaire to flee and to seek the protection of St.Ruadan of Lorrha, in today's County Tipperary, who had both the power and the determination to defy Diarmid's persistent requests for the surrender of the exiled king. Yet, even St. Ruadan found things difficult so Guaire fled across the sea to friends in Wales but again Diarmid too had powerful friends there so Guaire once more returned secretly to Ireland where he again stayed with St. Ruadan. Once more the High King declared that no holy man, no combarb, could be permitted to give sanctuary to a renegade and Guaire was snatched from sanctuary and taken as prisoner to Diarmid loaded with chains.(St. Ruadhan's well is to be found today south of the road that passes the present Church of Ireland cemetery in Lorrha, County Tipperary.)

Saint Ruadan was furious that anyone, even a High King , should so violate sanctuary. Such a precedent was dangerous to the safety of Mother Church. Consequently, Ruadan gathered about him the most holy men of the time: Saint Brendan of Birr, Molaise of the Western Isles, Saint Kevin of Glendalough and Saint Columba to resist the High King in his high-handedness. Before long, the whole of the Church in Ireland was ranged against the High King along with the chieftains whose sense of grievance found renewed expression. The holy men demanded of Diarmid not only Guaire's freedom but reassurance of the right of the monasteries to grant asylum without fear of violation. Not to be outdone, King Diarmid delivered a most eloquent speech explaining why it was necessary for the High King to be able to exercise his authority throughout the length and breadth of the country without hindrance. Prophetically he predicted the conflict which would arise in Ireland; the wars, the internal divisions and the anarchy when there was no central power to control the lesser kings. Such national unity under one High King was the lifelong ambition of the great Brian Boru but even he did not manage to achieve it. Diarmid's pleas made no difference to the holy men but in his turn Diarmid would not give way to them.

The holy men then fasted against Diarmid, an action considered to be most efficacious weapon used against anyone, kings included. That along with their cursing, a form of excommunication when the 'cursed' was denied the sacraments, was like the modern equivalent of using ballistic missiles. Diarmid's friends deserted him in great fear and all began to look upon him as a lost soul. Even his faithful guards "The Twelve Pillars of Tara" left his side as they too were fasted against. It should be remembered that the early druids of Ireland were feared for their lampoons and in their turn the holy men of Christianity, the natural successors of the ancient poets and druids, were also held in great awe by the populace.

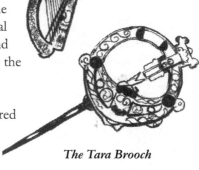

Finally the very hill of Tara, the revered historic meeting place of the Irish kings , was cursed as the holy men circled it, ringing bells and

The Tara Brooch

prophesying doom for the future Kings of Ireland who might dare to live there after Diarmid's defiance. At last the inevitable happened: Diarmid himself took fright and surrendered Guaire to the mercy of the Church. Unfortunately the power of the High Kings was now broken forever and Tara was destined to remain a desolate place ever afterwards.

The harp that once in Tara's halls, The soul of music shed,
Now hangs as mute on Tara's walls
As if that soul were fled.

Thus, according to the poets, King Guaire Aidhne was responsible not only for the demise of his own dynasty but also for the fall of Tara.

649 AD

Whatever the truth of the matter, Guaire certainly did fight several fierce battles against the High King Diarmid to prevent the encroachment of Munster, or to gain territory there himself. The battle against Diarmid, son of Aed Slaine, in which Guaire was so sorely defeated took place in 649 AD in Aidhne home territory near Gort, at Carn Conaill. (The High King was supposedly avenging St. Cellach). The place, Carn Conaill, commemorated Conaill, a Connaught warrior slain in single combat by the famous Cuchulain of the epic story 'The Cattle Raid of Cooley'. The Battle is mentioned in The Metrical Dindshenchas, (Poem 83, King Diarmid.)

The Book of the Dun (LV., Lebor na hUidre), a MS. from the end of the eleventh century commemorated it thus:

'Diarmait overcame Connaught till he came to Aidne. Guare gathered to him the men of Munster. These were the kings that came to succour Guare, to wit, Cuan, son of Enna, king of Munster, and Cuan, son of Conall, king of Hy Fidgenti, and Tolomnach, king of Hy LiatMin. The Guare was defeated, and a 'slaughter of chiefs' was inflicted there, including Cuan, son of Enna, king of Munster, and Cuan...'

Some annalists have suggested that Diarmid's attack was carried out as a chastisement of Guaire, who allegedly had deprived a woman, in religious life, of a cow, her only means of support. Such a dreadful action on the part of Guaire, famed fort his generosity and awarded the title of 'The Generous' certainly looks like a petty attempt at calumny. The most likely cause was a serious attempt by Diarmid to extract heavy tribute from the King of Connaught. Psychological warfare was no doubt as active in days gone by as it is today! Of course, with good reason, depicting the enemy as diabolical began with the story of Satan's rebellion against God! Throughout history and no doubt pre-history too demonising the enemy was a regular prelude to war.

Princely allies of Guaire's were killed in that battle; among them: Cuan, son of Enda, King of Munster, and Cuan, son of Conaill the chief of the Ui Fidgenti. Although Guaire lost the battle he is said to have won the peace by scoring a moral victory over King Diarmid. According to the Clonmacnoise version of the events, on the day before battle, Diarmid, visited the nearby monastery where he asked the good monks to pray for his safe return. For the spiritual favours promised, Diarmid would allow Clonmacnoise to assimilate the buildings and land of the smaller monastery of Liath Monchain. Anyone opposing the annexation would face the wrath of the High King. Three curses of the High King would then fall upon any subject of the King of Mide if he should so much as take a drink of water on that territory without permission of the monks of Clonmacnoise.

The High King then asked the monks if his body might eventually be buried within the grounds of their revered monastery. Getting God and his clerical representatives on side was also as popular then as it has been in latter centuries. Likely as not the Virgin Mary was petitioned aswell as in the conquest of the Albigensians, the sea battle Lepanto, on October 7, 1571 and so on.

On his behalf, Guaire sent the abbot of Clonfert, Cummene Fota, to ask Diarmid for a truce but the High King would not hear of it. He insisted upon battle. So much for the petitions of clergy working for the enemy! Subsequently a fierce struggle took place and Guaire lost. It must have been obvious to Diarmid that God was indeed on his side. Guaire then had to make a humiliating submission to Diarmid at sword point. This meant that the defeated king had to lie on the ground while the conqueror placed the tip of his sword between the teeth of the conquered. As it was the humiliation must have been hard for Guaire to bear but Diarmid had more punishment in store. He taunted Guaire for his legendary generosity by commanding a beggar, a jester and a leper to ask gifts of the bereft king. To everyone's surprise, Guaire asked permission to stand up in order to give the only thing he had left in the world - his shirt from his back! That action was certainly a good piece of one-up-man-ship on Guaire's part. To his credit Diarmid agreed to the request while congratulating Guaire in submitting to the greatest king of all, to God's Son, the King of Heaven! Peace was made between the two great men and Guaire was restored to his kingdom and his people. Would that today's conflicts cold be resolved like that!

For all his good intentions, Diarmaid and his brother Blathmac succumbed to a great plague, called the Buide Chonaill, which arrived in Ireland in 664.

King and Hermit Brother

It is likely that following his defeat in battle, Guaire was out of his kingdom for some time, for the poets have written that the king visited a hermit brother; a former warrior of Aidhne who had given up his martial career for the life of a hermit. King Guaire asks his brother, then living a life of solitary contemplation, to return to the life of a warrior and to help him shoulder the burdens of kingship but Marban refuses to do so. That encounter between the two brothers is celebrated in the poem *King and Hermit*. Written in the Tenth Century the verses are associated with a canticle *Benedicte Opere Domini Dominum* sung as part of the Office of Lauds in Ireland. Marban, brother of King Guaire, speaks in praise of the peace and tranquillity of the love of God expressed through the natural things of the woodland surrounding his hermitage.

The following is Kuno Meyer's translation but other versions have been written and it is possible that the scholar may prefer Gerard Murphy's translation with notes on the original Irish as given in Early Irish Lyrics. The poem is essentially lyrical, a song of praise for nature, but Guaire's comments suggest a world-weariness that comes from having to bear the cares of kingship. Several quatrains (stanzas of four lines) do not appear in the translation. It is possible they are more philosophical in kind. As it is, no doubt about it, this is a beautiful nature poem in its own right.

KING AND HERMIT

Guaire: Why, hermit Marvan, sleepest thou not
Upon a feather quilt?
Why sleepest thou abroad
Upon a pitchpine floor?

Marvan: I have a shieling in the wood,
None knows it save my God:
An ash tree on the hither side, a hazel bush beyond,
A huge old tree encompasses it.

Two heath clad doorposts for support
And a lintel of honeysuckle:
The forest around its narrowness sheds
Its mast upon fat swine.

The size of my shieling tiny, not too tiny,
And many are its familiar paths:
From its gable a sweet strain sings
A she-bird in her cloak of ousel's hue.

The stags of Oakridge leap
Into the river of clear banks:
Thence red Roiny can he seen,
Glorious Muckraw and Moinmoy.

A hiding mane of green-barked yew
Supports the sky:
Beautiful spot! The large green of an oak
Fronting the storm.

A tree of apples - great its bounty!
Like a hostel vast!
A pretty bush, thick as a fist, of tiny hazel-nuts,
A green mass of branches.

A choice pure spring and princely water
To drink:
There spring watercresses, yew-berries,
Ivy bushes thick as a man.

Around it, tame swine lie down,
Goats, pigs,
Wild swine, grazing deer,
A badger's brood.

A peaceful troop, a heavy host of denizens of the soil,
A-trysting at my house:
To meet them foxes come,
How delightful!

Fairest princes come to my house,
A ready gathering:
Pure water, perennial bushes,
Salmon, trout.

A bush of rowan, black, sloes,
Dusky blackthorns,
Plenty of food, acorns, pure berries,
Bare flags.

A clutch of eggs, honey delicious mast,
God has sent it:
Sweet apples, red whortleberries,
And blaeberries.

Ale with herbs, a dish of strawberries
Of good taste and colour,
Han's, berries of the juniper.
Sloes, nuts.

A cup with mead of hazel-nut, blue bells,
Quick-growing rushes,
Dun oaklets, manes of briar,
Goodly sweet tangle.

Guaire:
I would give my glorious kingship
With the share of my father's heritage -
To the hour of my death I would forfeit it
To be in the company, my Marvan.

Guaire' s Daughter Laments the Death of Dinertach

One source suggests that Guaire's allies in the battle of Cain Conaill included the Munster forces led by Cuan Mac Endai, King of Cashel; Cuan mac Conaill, King of Ui Fidgenti and also Tolomnach, King of Ui Leathain - each of whom was killed. The battle was historical fact and it must have been a very bloody one for so many princes to be killed on the same occasion. A seventh century poem suggests a strong link between Guaire and the Ui Fidgenti of Shannon. The poem is essentially a lament by Creide, a daughter of Guaire Aidhne, for Dinertach who was son of the king of the Ui Fidgenti. Dinertach had fought at Cam Conaill against Diarmid but had been wounded seventeen times through the breast of his tunic. He had fought with great valour in the 'Battle of Aidhne' but had died of his wounds after being carried from the field of battle. Creide had fallen in love with Dinertach but the young man had not survived the conflict at Cam Conaill and was buried, like so many princes at St. Colman's Church in the famous Aidhne monastery at Kilmacduagh. There is a pious tradition that the soil there around St. Colman's grave when applied to the faithful has a miraculous healing property.

The following version of the lament is once again from Kuno Meyer and it can he found in his book 'Ancient Irish Poetry', and another version may be found in the 'Faber Book of Irish Verse' – a translation by Alfred Perceval Graves.

THE SONG OF CREDE, DAUGHTER OF GUAIRE

These are arrows that murder sleep
At every hour in the bitter cold night;
Pangs of love throughout the day.
For the company of the man from Roiny.

Great love of a man from another land
Has come to me beyond all else:
It has taken my bloom, no colour is left.
It does not let me rest.

Sweeter than songs was his speech.
Save holy adoration of Heaven's King:
He was a glorious flame, no boastful word fell from his lips.
A slender mate for a maid's side.

When I was a child, I was bashful.
I was not given to going on trysts:
Since I have come to a wayward age,
My wantonness has beguiled me.

I have every good with Guaire,
The King of cold Aidhne:
But my mind has fallen away from my people
To the meadow at Irluchair.

There is chanting in the meadow of glorious Aidhne
Around the sides of Colman's Church;
Glorious flame, now sunk into the grave –
Dinertach was his name.

It wrings my pitiable heart, O chaste Christ.
What has fallen to my lot:
These are arrows that murder sleep
At every hour in the bitter cold night.

Guaire's Daughter and
Prince Cano of Scotland

Creide appears in another tragic legend,'Scela Cano meic Gartnain', (The Story of Cano mac Gartnain), in which she and Cano the son of King Gartnan of Scotland are the leading figures. The legend is an Irish version of the story of Tristan and Isolde. At the time of the story, Diarmid and Blathmac, his brother, are joint rulers of Ireland.

Again in this story the timing of events is a little faulty as Cano probably died in the year 688 AD so he was not likely to have been in Ireland at the time of the legend. An expedition from Scotland to Ireland did take place in 677 when presumably both Guaire and Diarmid were dead but the story is worth mention as there is some truth in the tale.

Aedan, a rival of Gartnan for the Kingship of Scotland, attacked the Isle of Skye where Gartnan lived. There, with the help of an army of 5000 men, Aedan killed his rival and all the inhabitants of the island. Cano, the son of Gartnan, who was being fostered,as the custom then was, away from the island was spared the slaughter and fled, with followers, to Ireland.

Once in Ireland, Diarmid and Blathmac received him warmly but when Aedan offered a huge reward of gold and silver to the Irish for the return of Cano, the young prince was convinced that his position had become dangerous. Meanwhile Diarmid's daughter had fallen in love with the Scottish prince and she had overheard the evil messengers of the infamous Aedan. She warned the young Cano that his life was in danger but Diarmid and Blathmac swore they had no intention of harming the prince. In fact, Blathmac persuaded Cano to pursue the returning messengers and to slay them once they were outside of the Irish Kings' territorial protection! Cano overtook the messengers at sea but allowed them to escape to Scotland without harm. Diarmid was so impressed by Cano's merciful actions that he prophesied the young man's successful accession to the Scottish throne.

Some time later Cano crossed the Shannon to visit Guaire and he arrived at the house of Marcan, the king of Ui Maine. (O'Kelly) . There lived Creide, daughter of Guaire, an unhappy wife of Marcan because the man was considerably older than she was. Cano's arrival thrilled her because she too had fallen in love with Cano on the strength of his reputation and what is more Cano had protected her some years ago when at the battle of Carn Conaill the Scottish prince had helped Diarmid against her father Guaire. On that occasion Cano's intervention had spared her harm.

Naturally, as a former enemy of Guaire, Cano was somewhat apprehensive of his visit to the King of Connaught, so Cano asked Creide's protection when he went to visit Guaire at his palace of Durlas at Kinvara. But there were other problems. Colcu, a son of Marcan's by a previous wife and now stepson of Creide's, strongly objected to his mother' association with Prince Cano. She nevertheless indiscreetly declared her love for the Scot quite openly and in the face of his objections.

Cano stayed at the palace of Dun Guaire for three months; during which time he and his retinue occupied one third of the fortress, Guaire and his courtiers occupied another third and the poet Senchan (Shanahan) along with his talented friends of the Great Visitation occupied the final third.

Now as Senchan and his friends lived with Guaire in great comfort and luxury he was a little put out by having to share hospitality with Cano and his friends, so he contrived to get Cano to leave by means of various plots. For example, while Cano and his men were out hunting, Senchan, by using magic, was able to confuse the hunters so that they frequently lost their way back. Before long, Cano's men insisted on leaving the enchanted place which so unnerved them. But before Cano and his followers left Kinvara to avail themselves of the hospitality of lllan, the son of Scannlan in Munster, Guaire treated them to a magnificent feast, a farewell party. Cano, Marcan, Colcu and all the noblemen of Connaught attended the banquet at which the beautiful Creide was allowed to pour the wine. So, like Grainne in the story 'The Pursuit of Diarmid and Grainne', Creide had drugged all the wine but her own and Cano's. A sleeping draught put all the guests asleep but the two lovers. She then entreated Cano to be her true and only love and to take her away with him, away from her old incapable husband. Cano was tempted but he refused to elope with her so long as he was a penniless mercenary: instead he asked her to wait until he had succeeded to the Scottish throne and then he would send for her to be his wife. As surety for his promise he gave Creide a stone, a vital thing which had come from his mother's mouth at his birth and within that stone lay Cano's life!

Stones in the mouth seem so improbable but in fact that physical phenomenon is not that rare. Tonsilloliths, or tonsil stones, may grow in the mouths of people suffering from acute tonsilitis. Some of these tonsilloliths, calcified debris, can be quite large, about half an inch across. It may be assumed that the protagonists in this story were truly amazed by the phenomenon and thereby attributed with lifegiving properties.

Once in Munster, Cano was royally received by Ilan, who in an attempt to outdo the legendary hospitality of the celebrated Guaire, gave Cano, every morning of his three year stay: three oxen, three salted pigs and a hundred and fifty loads of wood. Every evening the Scots were also given three vats of ale to help to pass the nights away in comfort.

Such a strain was put upon the forestlands of Ilan that people feared the daily supplies of firewood would soon destroy the woodlands! The woodlands, however, were spared for during that time a messenger arrived from Scotland to beg Cano to take up his kingship there at last. After receiving many more gifts from his host, Cano left Munster and his good Irish friend. Sad to say, a year after Cano had left, Ilan was slain and his fortress plundered by men of his own kindred. Legend has it that at the very time of Illan's death, Cano was out fishing off the west coast of his native land when a wave of blood washed against his vessel and Cano had a a premonition of Illan's death.

Cano took revenge upon Ilan's killers after landing in Ireland with a force of Saxons, Britons and Scots. He restored Ilan's son as king, taking hostages back with him to ensure the good behaviour of Ilan's enemies. While there he visited Creide but she was unable to escape with him.

Each year, Cano left Scotland to meet Creide at Inber Colptha, at the mouth of the River Boyne; but the suspicious Colcu was there on each occasion along with a hundred warriors to restrain the lovers. In an attempt to thwart Colcu, a secret tryst was arranged at Loch Creda. Creide travelled there, taking with her the sacred stone containing Cano's life. Meantime, Colcu had learned of the meeting, and in a rage he had intercepted Cano and had severely wounded the young king. On seeing the wounded Cano, his face covered with blood, Creide, in dismay, fell on the slippery rocks shattering her head at the same time dropping the precious stone which broke as she fell. The unfortunate Cano died at sea on his way back to his beloved Scotland.

In his time Guaire's rule extended south into Thomond and that rule included power and influence in Corcomruad and in Corco Baiscind, south west Clare, in contention with the Ui Fidgenti and the Dal Cais or Dalcassians from whom descended the last High King of Ireland - Brian Boru, son-in-law of Mulroy O'Hynes. It is thought that Guaire's failure to hold those territories seriously weakened the subsequent fortunes of the Aidhne in later years.

The Great Visitation of Poets to Dun Guaire

Senchan and his followers, mentioned in the previous story, were indeed a burden upon Guaire at the time of Cano's visit. The arrogant Senchan along with his 300 poet friends and their families arrived at Guaire's palace on a 'Great Visitation' to test the King's generosity to the limit. Any weakness in Guaire's generosity was to be ridiculed through the poets' satirical talents. In those days a 'bad press' from the poets was supposed to bring out shameful blotches on the faces of their victims who were, traditionally, kings. Fear of ridicule was so great that kings went to extraordinary lengths to avoid the sharp ends of poets' tongues. One could compare it with today's politicians at the mercy of vituperative press barons!

An early Modern Irish tale of 'Guaire's Troublesome Guest Company' is a burlesque of the extravagant behaviour of a band of poets who stayed with Guaire all those years ago. Although W.B. Yeats made Senchan Torpeist, the hero in the play 'The King's Threshold' about a bard's hunger strike, the ancient Irish tales make him a great nuisance.

According to ancient legend, after Senchan Torpeist had been elected chief of the Irish poets, he persuaded his fellow bards to visit Guaire whose fabled generosity had so far been above reproach. They agreed to attempt to find a weakness in Guaire's patience and to exploit it in order to lampoon this King of Connaught. At the time Guaire's hill fort must have been a great deal bigger than the present castle of the O'Hynes, which of course was actually built some eight hundred years later, in Tudor times. The 'Book of Lecan' describes Guaire's palace of Kinvara (There was another at Gort and another near the Moy) as a 'white-sheeted fort of soft stones', a dwelling for poets and bishops. The fortification may have been covered in the same kind of white quartz used on the façade of the ancient Newgrange megalithic passage tomb in Nowth, north of Dublin which must have looked very impressive in bright sunlight.

Only a substantial residence could have housed the retinue of poets during the 'Great Visitation' and the Dun Guaire must have been eminently suited to the occasion. To accommodate these special guests Guaire had an extra special house built there; a house with eight sides, with eight beds along each side and lower beds in front of each of them. There were wells for the mens' morning ablutions and separate wells for the women of the Company. Fresh spring water flowed through the rooms with the wells. Interestingly to this very day, fresh water travelling underground from Coole Park Lake, bubbles up in the sea water near the present Dunguaire castle!

During the stay of 'The Troublesome Guest Company' masses of foodstuffs were regularly gathered to feed the demanding multitude exercising fastidious tastes. In all, there were 150 major poets, 150 minor poets, 150 hounds, 150 servants, 150 women and 27 men of every craft to cater for the wishes of the guests. The number 150 must have had a special mystical significance among the Irish. In fact the fifteen mysteries of the rosary, 150 Hail Marys, originated in the monasteries of the early Irish church arising out of the recitation by monks of the 150 psalms of David. Lay people adopted and adapted the practice for themselves thus inventing the Rosary long before St.Bernard ever thought about it!

King Guaire welcomed them all and made available whatever delicacies took their fancy, but, despite the hospitality the poets grumbled and complained incessantly, finding fault with everything they could. This was wrong - that was wrong. This was too sweet - that was too bitter.

Muirenn, the widow of Senchan's predecessor groaned with longing. She was desperate said she for a bowl of new milk set with the marrow of a pig's trotter. Along with it she longed for a pet cuckoo to sing in a tree beside her although 'the time was out of season' as it was between Christmas and Little Christmas. She longed, too, to ride a roan horse wearing a cloak made of spiders' webs while on her back should be tied a full load of lard melted down from the body of a white boar! Thus attired, she wanted to ride into Durlas in great triumph happily humming a tune! Such was her immoderate desire and her requests were typical of the absurd demands of the troublesome guests.

Guaire, of course, was astounded by her absurd wishes and pointed out just how impossible it would be to fulfil them. In desperation, the good king prayed to heaven for God's help in meeting the harridan's unruly wishes.

Fortunately for Guaire, his brother Marban, Marvan, a hermit, called on him and on hearing of the incorrigible woman's demands resolved to help Guaire. The holy Marban, who had given up an aristocratic life, lived in poverty as a swineherd had a large white boar of which he was particularly proud and since the lard would have to come from his favourite pet he swore 'vengeance' on Muirenn and on the troublesome guest company for thus causing the death of the boar. It is hardly appropriate to attribute a holy man with a desire for vengeance, surely his action would be more in the nature of teaching her a salutary lesson.

All was accomplished. Muirenn had her wish but as it so happened as she was riding along adorned in this ridiculous manner, her horse tripped and she was thrown to the ground and instantly killed. The proverb "A hag's load of lard" is said to have its origins in the episode.

Other importunate demands were made to test Guaire's hospitality to the limits of his ingenuity. Among the unreasonable and indeed unseasonable demands was one from Medb, the daughter of Senchan. She wanted blackberries out of season - right in the middle of winter! Senchan himself satirized the mice which ate the eggs that he was too fussy to consume. He then satirized the cats for not catching the mice which had offended him! The King of Cats was so incensed that he carried Senchan off on his back but fortunately for Senchan, if not for Guaire, as they were passing Clonmacnoise. St. Ciaran rescued the poet. Not to be outdone, and as the saint was a friend of Guaire's. Senchan cursed the saint too for preventing his death which could thus have been blamed upon Guaire!

While Senchan was returning from Clonmacnoise, Marban had entered the poets' chambers deliberately entering by a door which sent an importunate blast of cold air all over the fussy poets. He was very angry and was determined to make things awkward for them. Senchan arrived back to agree with Marban that the holy man might choose any form of music from the assembled poets as took his fancy. Upon hearing this, Marban demanded of them an especially exhausting form of humming called 'cronan snagach' and before long the 27 hummers lay prostrate with fatigue. On Marban's repeated requests for a continuation of the humming, an 'ollam' (a wise man or professor), Dael, from Leinster, suggested an alternative entertainment in which Marban was set some very tricky riddles which were supposed to make him look foolish. But to everyone's surprise and delight he answered them perfectly including the four:

What good did man find on earth that God did not find?
Which two trees lose their leaves only when they die?
What beast lives in the sea and drowns when taken out of it?
What animal is burned when taken out of the fire?

Marban answered:

Man found a worthy master in God.
The trees are the holly and the yew.
The beast is Grim Abraein.
The animal is the salamander.

The Epic Poem
'The Cattle Raid of Cooley'
is 'Resurrected'

Realising he had been beaten, the Leinster poet retired ignominiously from the contest leaving Marban very much in command. Marban went on to insist upon a resumption of the humming but each poet, in his turn, played for time by matching his wits against the holy man and each in turn was humiliated by the hermit. Senchan himself took up the humming and each time he stopped for breath the King's brother made him go on until the very effort of humming caused one of the poet's eyes to pop out of its socket onto his cheeks! Fortunately for him, the holy man's powers were available, as Marban was able to replace the eye! Guaire was none too pleased with his brother's attempts to discomfort the guests but Marban insisted again and again that the humming continue.

In a brave attempt to win the day for the poets, Fis, son of Fochmhairi (Knowledge, Son of Enquiry), offered to tell a story because he was the best storyteller in the whole of Ireland. But he too reeled under the impact of Marban's requests as the hermit asked for Táin Bó Cúailnge, an Ulster epic which had been forgotten after the manuscript had been taken abroad and exchanged for the Culmen, Isidore of Seville's 'Etymologiae'. (Apparently this was an allegorical reference to the substitution of native Irish mythology by monastic Latin). Marban insisted upon being told the story and what was more, he put them all under a spell until they could tell him the tale in full. He made it impossible for any of the poets to compose a poem of any kind until the tale had been told.

Filled now with great consternation, the poets begged their leave of Guaire, who, in his turn begged them to stay even though they had lost their poetic gifts. Senchan allowed the women and children to stay with the king but he expressed his complete disdain for mere charity and left with his poets to search for the Tain Bo, The Cattle Raid of Cooley, probably the best known work of Irish Literature.

On meeting a leper on their journey to stay with the king of Leinster, the poets were chided by the man for seeking a king's hospitality while their poetic gifts were in abeyance and they were unable to render service for their bread and board. The leper promised Senchan a poem which might be useful on their journey but first the chief poet had to kiss the leper. Filled with great horror Senchan, nevertheless, complied with the leper's wish and armed thus with a useful bartering tool, a new poem, the poets went on their way.

Their search took them to Scotland, for try as they might to find the Tain Bo in Ireland, they could not. On the voyage to Scotland, they passed the Isle of Man where they were hailed by a woman calling from a clifftop. They wanted to land on the island to break their journey but were prevented from landing until they had swapped verses with the strange woman. Their newly acquired poem was proving to be very useful indeed! And so too was the talent of the leper who had decided to travel with them.

So enchanted was the woman with the company and with the verse swapping that she gave the bereft poets half her fortune of 60 marks, amassed by her by healing the sick and selling salt made from sea water. The money would be useful in paying their way through Scotland.

But ill luck pursued them, for nowhere throughout the whole of Scotland were the unhappy poets able to find any living soul who could recite the Tain Bo for them. They were obliged to return crestfallen to their native Ireland with all the marks of defeat.

On arriving in Dublin at the end of their fruitless search, the poets were greeted by Senchan's brother who, unknown to them at the time had appeared to them during their journey as the leper who had helped them from time to time. Fortunately for Senchan, this brother of his was Saint Caillin who told them that now they had learned some humility the hard way they should return to Durlas and beg Marban to tell them how they might learn the Tain Bo.

This they did and Marban revealed the awful truth; only the dead Fergus MacRoich had known the epic but he had been buried years ago. [Fergus mac Róich, the son of 'great horse', a qondam king of Ulster, played a leading role in the Ulster cycle of Mythology and was an alleged lover of Queen Maeve of Connaught.]

The despair and lamentations of the poets were pitiable to behold and the hermit Marban was moved to help them. He gathered together the saints of Ireland and together they went to the grave of the dead Fergus. There, they fasted for three days and called upon Christ to raise Fergus from the grave. The poets watched with astonishment and awe as the figure of Fergus stepped from the earth before them. He then recited the long forgotten poem while St. Ciaran wrote it down on the hide of the Dun Cow. After Fergus had returned to his final resting place, the whole company, filled with gratitude for the great gift they had been given, returned to Kinvara, to Durlas, where, much to Guaire's delight, the Tain Bo was once again recited by the poets of Ireland. Marban then rebuked the poets and would not let them leave again until they promised that each poet would return to his own territory and that they would never gather again to make a Great Visitation to any king throughout the land. And they never did! The story symbolizes the end of the old Gaelic order.

According to tradition the poets stayed with King Guaire for "... a year, a quarter and a month" and before they left, in fact, before they left for Scotland, they dedicated a poem to the hospitable Guaire.

We depart from thee, O stainless Guaire,
A year, a quarter and a month
Have we sojourned with thee, O king.
Three times fifty poets, good and smooth,
Three times fifty students in the poetic art,
Each with a servant and a dog.
They were all fed in the one great house;
Each man had his separate meal,
Each man had his separate bed
We never arose at early morning
Without contentions, without calming.
I declare to thee, O God,
Who canst the promise verify,
That should we return to our own lands
We shall visit thee again. O Guaire, tho' now we depart.

WHITE SHEETED FORT OF SOFT STONES

Although the early Irish preferred living in crannog-like dwellings of timber, branches and grasses, they did build in stone as witnessed by the many souterrains (underground strongholds) and ring forts of ancient times so perhaps much of Durlus Guaire was stone-built and possibly faced with the same kind of sparkling white quartzite stones as Newgrange, in County Meath, constructed over 5,000 years ago, one of the archaeological wonders of western Europe. Newgrange was 'white sheeted' and so also was Dun Guaire. The old name of Durlas or Durlus meant a 'strong fort' so it is not surprising to learn that the coat of arms of Guaire's descendants bears the words 'TURRIS FORTIS' or strong fort. Furthermore, the Book of Lecan refers to the ancient palace as 'Rath Durlais', a fort of everlasting fame. It was: The white sheeted fort of soft stones, Habitation of poets and bishops, as mentioned by Colgan in a poem by Giolla Iosa MacFirbis to O'Dowd of the northern Ui Fiachrach Aidhne in 1417.

Whatever its structure, King Guaire's palace must have been a very large residence, to have housed the great retinue of poets during the 'Great Visitation' of Senchan, the poet and his great retinue and certainly much bigger than the present Tudor tower house.

An eighth century law tract 'Crith Gabbach' lays down the minimum dimensions for a king's dun or fortress and its eventual size reflected the power of the monarch and his ability to command a large work force. The walls should be at least seven score feet along each direction. The moat surrounding the dun should be at least seven feet wide and twelve feet deep. Close by would he the house for the royal entourage and it would be at least thirty feet long and about the same distance wide. It would be built about twelve feet away from the king's residence.

Each of the clerics in service in the royal palace who undertook domestic duties would be entitled to a wagon load of rushes at regular intervals together with a wagonload of firewood. Should the King become a pilgrim then he was entitled, not to a fort, but to a house, thirty-seven feet long with twelve bed cubicles only. One source states that King Guaire had a special guest house built for his visiting poets and that wells supplied running water for his guests ablutions. Obviously some ingenious ancient builders must have channelled the springs of fresh water, which, to this very day, bubble up around the castle of Dun Guaire.

The same law tract lays down rules about the King's weekly duties:

'Sunday was for entertaining and the drinking of ale; Monday was for legal business; Tuesday was devoted to the playing of chess; Wednesday was set aside for the racing of greyhounds; Thursday was to be spent on domestic affairs concerned with the King's own family; Friday was for horse racing and Saturday for making judgments according to the laws of the Kingdom.'

King Guaire and Saint Colman

Every year, visitors pass through Kinvara on their way to the unique 'desert' of limestone called 'the Burren'. Botanists from all over the world arrive to study the floral peculiarities of the region. There during the Stone Age, a process of clearance began and it continued so that in the course of time, the dry, wooded uplands were denuded of trees leaving the stark, almost frightening bare rock.

In Cromwell's day, the inordinate tree felling in the region created bogs where good pasture once lay. Protestant settlers were given land along a five mile coastal strip but they tended to leave the Burren alone after the Cromwellian, Ludlow, who, in 1651, slaughtered women and children in the O'Shaughnessy castle in Gort, described the Burren as ... a savage land, yielding neither water enough to drown a man, nor a tree to hang him, nor soil enough to bury him". Thus, in terms of killing, a murderous soldier described the place. Yet there is water there, in plenty, but it is hidden away in underground rivers showing itself only occasionally as springs. There are swallow holes, places where living streams drop into underground caverns aplenty. Limestone pavements are to be found everywhere in this region of Yugoslavian 'karst'.

Moist sea airs blow gently over the area from the Atlantic Ocean, - over clefts and runnels of rock, where, on a light sprinkling of soil are to be found myriads of wild flowers; blue Spring Gentians; pink Irish Close-Flowered Orchid; Hoary Rock rose; Sandwort; dark red Helleborine; Shrubby Cinquefoil and so many more. The remains of the African Wild Cat have been found there and the bones of Irish Elk, wolves and bears. In fact, today, the visitor can see the remains of bears which roamed the hills during Guaire's reign by calling at the Aillwee (Yellow) Cave, a most attractive tourist spot lying two miles south-east of Ballyvaughan just off the Ennis Road. The cave was formed millions of years ago and today the visitor may be conducted through beautiful stalagmites and stalactites formed within the caverns of the underground river.

There too, in the Burren, some 4 miles to the south-west, may be found the remains of the hermitage in which long ago, the brother or cousin of King

Guaire lived for seven years. This holy man who eventually founded the monastery of Kilmacduagh, was born into the princely race of Dathy. His father was Duac, son of Cell mac Duath and eighth descendant of Dathy, the King of Ireland before St. Patrick's time. The place is difficult to find but certainly worth discovering.

Once again, legend and history have been interwoven in the accounts of his life, so that the stories about him have been elaborated in the telling. Before his birth, it was prophesied that his fame would surpass all others of the distinguished line of the Ui Fiachrach Aidhne. Apparently, on hearing this, Colman, the King of Connaught, father of Guaire, became so jealous that he sought the death of the unborn child and his mother Rhinach, the only daughter of Cormac. Needless today, Rhinach went and hid herself in the great wood of the Burren and the child was born there, in Corker, under an ash tree. It is said that she was seized by the king's servants and was cast into the river of Kiltart with a heavy stone tied around her neck. She was miraculously preserved from death and the stone may still be seen on the windowsill of a ruined chapel near the river edge to this day!

Tradition tells us that while the mother waited anxiously for someone to baptise her infant son, two aged and infirm clerics approached, and, upon praying for water with which to christen the child, a miraculous fountain gushed up from the earth. The child was baptised and the pilgrims were cured of blindness and lameness. That particular holy well, (There are others nearby!) bearing the saint's name, may be found at Corker, where, at the turn of this century, the local people sought effective cures. Is it possible that the "cure for all evil between the two mill wheels of Ballylee" which so intrigued the poet Yeats was the water flowing from the well?

When old enough, the child was sent in secret to Aranmore on the western islands where he grew in wisdom through prayer and mortification returning to the mainland later and in secret to live the frugal life of the 7th Century hermit. In the solitude of the Burren, he lived within the woods and upland crags with one disciple as companion and mass server. Their home was a cave beneath Eagles' Rock set in the escarpment called Cinn Aille not far from Keelhilla. Nearby was a pleasant fountain of crystal clear water which provided drink for them while their food was sprigs of cress, berries and the occasional wild fowl. Bears and other wild creatures roamed the, woods and the warm wet winds blew in from the sea only five miles away. There, he built a small oratory and St. Colman mac Duagh said mass on a limestone altar with the disciple as mass server throughout the year and throughout the changing seasons.

THE MIRACLE OF THE DISHES

One day, a most remarkable thing happened to forge a lasting link between the palace of Dun Guaire and the hermitage home of St. Colman at Tobar mac Duach. On a certain Easter Sunday morning near the end of the saint's long sojourn in the wilderness, the priest and the disciple sat down to a frugal meal of barley bread, wild herbs, watercress and spring water dressed as they were in simple deerskin clothes. They were close to starvation as they had had little to eat throughout the winter. The disciple, feeling very sorry for himself, truculently remarked that their meal would be quite different from the succulent banquet which at that very moment smoked on the table of King Guaire at the palace of Durlas such a short distance away.

He was right, for in the usual lavish style of the king's palace, a sumptuous feast had been spread on the board; a boar and a stag cooked whole and brought to the table on huge trenchers, were the centrepiece of a great array of delicacies!

Meanwhile in the little hermitage, St. Colman's disciple gazed for a while at his meagre meal and said:"It's no use. I'm famished and I'm going to Durlas to ask for food".

St. Colman, feeling very sorry for his companion, promised that soon they would be supplied with an excellent Easter dinner. "Stay here with me and I will see if I can procure a worthy feast for you just where you sit." He knelt down in prayer.

Coincidentally, back in Dun Guaire when everything was laid ready for the banquet and all the guests were seated, King Guaire prayed that if it so pleased God the banquet might be set out before His servants who might have greater need of it than his present company did. Whereupon, at the very moment he stopped praying, the guests watched in horror and amazement as the dishes, trenchers and methers, boar and stag, floated up from the table and passed through doors and windows borne aloft by invisible hands to be whisked away towards the Burren. Not so much was left on the table as would feed a wolf dog!

Guaire and his retinue mounted their horses in great haste and followed closely by footmen and dogs, all, made off in hot pursuit after the disappearing dishes and their Easter feast! During their pursuit the royal pursuants watched the dishes gradually come to ground in front of the two wildest looking men they had ever seen!

As the servant was about to eat from the remarkable answer to prayer, he looked up to see the hillside covered with angry men on horseback galloping fiercely towards him. He was terrified and said so adding that he could not settle to eat in peace in the circumstances. Saint Colman answered: "Eat in peace. There is no danger, for it is my brother – the king and his household and I will take care they do not interrupt you!"

At once, the horses' hooves, footmen's feet and dogs' legs were held fast in the ground so that not one of them could move!

It wasn't until after the disciple had eaten his fill, that the saint released the pursuers and the king got close enough to recognise Colman. Overcome with joy at the discovery of his kinsman and wishing to make amends for his father's hostility, King Guaire prevailed upon Colman to become Bishop of the Kingdom of Ui Fiachrach Aidhne. With great reluctance, because of his humility, Saint Colman agreed to this request as he came to see it as the will of God.

Colman and his monks set to work to build a monastery on the site now called Kilmacduagh (Church of Mac Duagh). The king sent teams of oxen and hundreds of labourers to help the holy men and tradition has it that the construction was supervised by an illiterate but very practical monk called Gobban who had been sent along by St. Madoc of the Fens.

The marks left in the ground by the horses' hooves and the dogs' paws can be seen to this day on Bothar na mias (Bohernameece) or The Road of the Dishes. The tracks are actually curious weatherings made in the limestone by water erosion over the years but they are remarkably like what they are supposed to be and the local people will confirm that all those years ago something very remarkable happened there so why should it not be as tradition tells it?

The small limestone cave in which the saint lived for so long may still be found in Keelhilla at the foot of Slieve Carran about four and a half miles from Kinvara to the south-west. The hermitage and Tober mac Duagh, the well used by the saint are actually just inside County Clare in the scree at the base of Eagles' Rock in a wild rocky area. (The visitor will find T.D. Robinson's excellent topographical map 'The Burren' invaluable in locating the site.)

In that place too can be found Saint Macduach's Bed (the cave), Saint Macduagh's Church, the ruins of a small oratory and two small altars. A quarter of a mile away to the south-east of these is the grave of Saint Colman's servant and nearby, the Road of the Dishes. The place has an atmosphere all of its own, an eerie spot, even today in broad daylight. The bare karstic rock has a beauty which is unique and the myriads of wild flowers are a delight.

The hermitage became a traditional pilgrimage place visited on the saint's day, 3 February, although some place the saint's birthday on October 29. It is said that this Saint Colman was born in the year 623 AD, and was certainly in Guaire's time.

Many of the Irish monastic saints were attributed with special powers over animals and in this respect Saint Colman mac Duagh was no exception as legend has it that a cock woke him for night office, a mouse prevented him from sleeping after it and a fly kept his place in a book! At least two of these creatures are depicted in the magnificent mural of Saint Colman which adorns the wall of a side chapel in the new cathedral of Our Lady Assumed into Heaven and St. Nicholas in Galway City. That fresco was painted by Aengus Buckley, OP, and sponsored by Dr. Michael Browne was presented at the cathedral on the occasion of the visit of Terence Cardinal Coole, Archbishop of New York on the 4 August, 1970. A plaque commemorates the event with a dedication, 'In prayerful gratitude to the people of Galway from your relatives and friends at St. Patrick's Cathedral. The fresco shows St. Colman in the ceremonial robes of a bishop in the company of a cowled monk, his companion together with several other figures with the famous Round Tower of Kilmacduagh rising behind them all and a jolly rooster in the foreground.

SOME STRANGE HAPPENINGS ASSOCIATED WITH SAINT COLMAN

In the past the Feast of Saint Colman was regarded as a very solemn one, on the vigil of which it was considered grievously sinful to eat meat, eggs or milk diets. Several stories exist which illustrate the dire consequences of breaking the vigil. Colgan, in the 17th Century wrote that when dining with the Earl of Kildare, William O'Shaughnessy forgot about the vigil and upon receiving the meat dish was surprised to find it covered with fresh blood and uneatable. A replacement dish of freshly cooked meat turned up the same way and that too could not be eaten.

On another occasion when workmen were threshing corn on the vigil of St. Colman, they refused the vigil diet asking instead for white meats. However when Lady O'Shaughnessy supplied the milk dish demanded by the workmen, the liquid turned to blood. It appears that the workmen were eventually convinced of the folly of their ways in breaking the vigil of the holy man's feast day.

Towards the close of the eighteenth century, a Protestant farmer called Faircloth wanted to plant some wheat on St. Colman's day but his labourers were unwilling to help him. The farmer himself nevertheless planted the wheat which grew abundantly at the end of the growing period. However when put to the sickle the many ears were found to hold no grain!

Another tradition tells of the thwarting of robbers at Kilmacduagh. Farmers, fearing their herds would be stolen, drove their flocks onto land close to St. Colman's cemetery. Then when the robbers attempted to drive the cattle away they could not, for, when the robbers were in the cemetery they thought the cattle were outside and when outside the cemetery the robbers thought the cattle were inside! The robbers then gave up the attempt.

Colgan recounts another story which describes how a hangman tied a noose about the neck of a man who had placed some miraculous wood from St. Colman's tree in his mouth to gain the saint's intervention. Although the man hung as though dead on being cut down he was found to be alive. He was hanged again and again without ensuing death until the hangman found the wood, took it from the man's mouth and the hapless victim died on the next hanging. Fahey cites O'Flaherty as having witnessed a man, tormented by a thorn in his eye, lying down on Colman's grave in Kilmacduagh and getting up after the thorn had suddenly disappeared!

THE WELLS OF ST. COLMAN

There once was a holy well in Kilmacduagh, still discernible in 1893, at which many cures were effected and there was a small boy of some five years of age who was preserved from drowning. The boy had wandered away from his parents and unknown to them had fallen headfirst into the well. After some time the boy was found head downwards but alive although his head was under water! On being questioned the boy said he had been looked after by a venerable old man with white hair! This well is probably the one found in Corker, Kiltartan, today.

Other Colman wells could be found: one in Oughtmama, County Clare, said to have cured eyes; another, curing eyes and backs, near St. Colman's Hermitage at Eagle's Rock, Slievecarran, a mile south of the ruins of Kilmacduagh; another at Caherglissane about 3 miles south-east of Kinvara; yet another in the parish of Kilbecanty; one on the eastern shore of Lough Cutra; another in the parish of Kilchrist and yet another, marked with a small stone cross, near the ruins of the old palace of Guaire at Kinvara, at Dunguaire. There is no doubt that in past centuries before modern medicine and surgery, sheer desperation in the face of sickness led people to hope for cures at holy sites. Likewise tens of thousands of people still visit Lourdes and Fatima today filled with hope for miraculous cures.

In the mid-nineteenth century the well, Tubber Mac Duach, Carrowroe, was but a small spring of water walled in and shaded by hawthorns, near a withered ash. In Colman's time it was probably a baptismal font. There was a stile set in thewall for access by pilgrims. A Mr. Sheehan, who lived nearby erected a stone cross over the wall.

Tubber-macduagh St. Colman's Well,
Kinvara, as it would have looked
in the 1890s.

The Monastery at Kilmacduagh

King Guaire certainly donated the land upon which the monastery was built. Legend tells us that the choice of site was left to Providence so that, one day, as Saint Colman was passing through the great wood of the Burren, his cincture, belt, fell to the ground and upon that place was built the monastery which stands there today. Throughout the centuries the cincture, the belt, was jealously guarded by the O'Shaughnessys but it seems to have been lost in the nineteenth century, or even earlier, perhaps at the Battle of the Boyne, where it was carried by the O'Shaughnessys during the conflict. The belt, studded with gems, would fit only those who were chaste. The impure could not be fitted with the girdle no matter how slim their waists.

Mosaic over doorway to St. Colman's
Church in Gort, county Galway.

The remains of the good saint's crozier, used in the earlier centuries to give solemn sacred sanction to treaties, may now be seen in the National Museum of Ireland in Dublin. Only part of the shaft has survived because over the years much of it has broken away and been lost. All that is left is a portion of the original wooden shaft within an ornamental casing, much elaborated and restored during the centuries since it lay in the hands of the bishop himself. The 'shrine', the casing, is made of bronze with four knops, described by the National Museum thus, "...three of which are decorated with geometric patterns originally outlined with niello. The shrine is of the late 11th Century or the early 12th". According to The Annals of the Four Masters, in the year 1223 AD, Seannusagh Macgiollananee O'Shaughnusy was killed by Clan Cuiein (MacNamaras), who carried off the great crozier of St. Colman of Macduagh "a deed by which the Bachal Mor of St. Colman, son of Duagh, was profaned". (It would appear that the MacNamaras had broken an oath sworn on the crozier, hence the profanation). The crozier too, like the girdle, had been studded with gems and coated with gold.

St. Colman's crozier, now housed in the National Museum of Ireland.

After Mansfield's judgment against the O'Shaughnessys, the crozier passed into the hands of a family allied to the Butlers of Cregg upon the marriage of Helen, sister of Colonel William O'Shaughnessy to Theobald Butler. Then after the ruin of the Gort baronets, the crozier remained in the hands of the Butlers and in those times the relic was used to induce defrauders to give up their ill-gotten gains. Monsignor Fahey, who wrote the History and Antiquities of Kilmacduagh mentions that he once met an old man, John Keane of Gort, who borrowed the crozier from the Cregg family for this very purpose.

Mary Cahill of the Irish Antiquaries Division of the Museum quotes from an article by H.S. Crawford in the Journal of the Royal Society of Antiquaries where it is given that the crozier was purchased from the last of its keepers, the O'Heynes by Dr. Petrie. Margaret Stokes confirms this in Early Christian Art in Ireland saying that it was indeed obtained from the O'Heynes who succeeded the O'Shaughnessys as custodians.

St. Colman with friends and companions. Sketch of
mural in Galway Cathedral.

Saint Colman's choice of site for his church and monastery was a very
practical one as his new diocese met the needs of the tribal territories of
the Ui Fiachrach Aidhne because his Diocese of Kilmacduagh was co-
extensive with the lands ruled by the chieftains of the O'Heyne, 'one of
the noblest tribes of ancient Erin' (Monsignor Fahey). The O'Heyne votive
church is still conspicuous among the present ruins of the ecclesiastical
buildings on a site lying three miles south-west of Gort to the north-west
of the main Gort-Corrofin road. Close to a lough, with beautiful views
across to the Burren, there stands a group of ruined buildings overlooked
by a tall round tower similar to the one at Glendalough - only this one, the
tallest in Ireland, leans two feet out of true
perpendicular!

The monastery at Kilmacduagh was founded after the grant of land by
King Guaire, and, in its most active time between the seventh and early
sixteenth century, it contributed much towards the learning and culture of

early Ireland. The Irish cathedral church surrounded by a diocese favoured the growth of learning as it strengthened the Celtic tradition of a privileged scholarly class originally based on druid power and replaced in time by the power of the austere men of Christianity. Ireland became the 'insula sanctorum et doctorum', that is the island of the holy and the learned.

The cathedral church of Templemore mac Duach occupies the site of the original building which was a simple oblong lit by a single window at the east end and several more windows along the southern side. It is thought that Colman's first church must have been destroyed by Danes and rebuilt together with other buildings on the site under the patronage of Brian Boru who had married Mor O'Heyne, daughter of Mulroy O'Heyne.

The elaborate Gothic doorway was built during the 14th. and 15th. centuries at a time when the original western entrance had been filled with rubble to seal it off. The side chapels were added in the form of a Greek cross with the Lady Chapel on the right. While on the left is the O'Shaughnessy chapel, a mortuary chapel for that family, who were also descendants of Guaire and for a long time Guardians of the crozier and the girdle of Saint Colman.

Against the gable end is an altar-like tomb, above which is a set of entablature placed for safekeeping into the wall. One of these shows the O'Shaughnessy arms of the triple-towered castle supported by lions on either side. There is also a quaint Crucifixion scene with 'clothes peg' arabesque figures on either side. One of the reliefs shows Saint Colman holding a large crozier. On a nearby door lintel has been carved a crude 'comic' face at some time or other. This tomb may be that of Sir Dermot O'Shaughnessy and his ancestors, referred to as 'the tomb where my ancestors were buried' in his will of 18 January 1671. A large slab, one of many set into the floor, is inscribed with the request to 'Pray for the soul of Garret Hynes and his posterity this monument was erected by his son Dominick Hynes A.D. 1803'.

On the side of the road opposite the cathedral church, hard up against the wall of the road, is Templemurry, St. Mary's Church, the oldest church of the group on the site. Part of it dates back to the 13th Century. It measures about 41 feet and the inside walls are somewhat splayed.

On the southwest side of the cathedral was the mortuary chapel, Leaba Mic Duagh, the burial place of Saint Colman although it is said that his body was later reburied in Aughrim. Dr. French, a more recent bishop of the diocese, was also buried there in 1852 and the spot was marked with a memorial cross placed there by Dr. MacCormack, Monsignor Fahey and their friends. According to Bishop Pococke, a small 'cell' occupied the site as late as 1752.

To the north by north-east of both the cathedral church and St. John's Chapel lies a square building which has recently been restored. It was the Abbot's House, or Glebe House, built in the 14th or 15th Centuries and used not only as the abbot's residence but as a seminary for postulant priests. It is a fortified tower house with gun loops. The upper floor had an oriel from which, it is thought, the bishop would bless the pilgrims who visited the site in large numbers. A small square projection on the south-west side may have been a guard tower at one time. In an article for the Royal Society of Antiquaries of Ireland, J. Fahey likens the masonry to that in the ruined O'Heynes/O'Shaughnessy Castle at Ardrahan which had been built in the 13th Century.

Close to Glebe House, there is a car park and a lane which leads to a building containing some of the more interesting remains, the O'Heynes Abbey. This building is a listed National Monument and its plaque reads: 'O'Heynes Church. This church was built for the Augustine Canons in the early 13th Century by Owen O'Heyne, Lord of the district, who died in in 1253. The stonework of the decorated chancel arch and the east window is among the best of Connacht and belongs to the school of Kilfenora and Corcomroe. Part of the nave of the church collapsed in the 15th Century and was replaced by a wall inside it. The Canons stayed on until around 1584.'

The Canons Regular of Augustine were established at Kilmacduagh by Bishop Ileyan and it was probably wrecked in the beginning of the 13th Century by William Fitz Adelm de Burgo to revenge his defeat at Kilmacduagh at the hands of Cathal the Red-handed O'Connor. It was, however, rebuilt later by the Canons and became known as Teampuill Muinter Heyne because the O'Heyne were the patrons, or 'herenachs' of this monastery. It is likely that the Rules followed by the monks there were those of Colman's friend and mentor, Saint Columba. The work is described as cyclopean with medieval Irish. The walls of the monastery chapel still stand with part of the domestic quarters still in place and used as a mausoleum by the patrons.

Curious visitors today taking the trouble to place a small boulder to stand on to look through a narrow window of the mausoleum in the O'Heyne Church may look into a sealed chamber within which may seen a leaden coffin of a nineteenth century Protestant landlord, Taylor, Esquire, possibly Walter Shawe-Taylor. The sepulchral site is unmarked probably because, to say the least, he made himself very unpopular during the Famine! A descendant of his, Frank Shawe-Taylor was ambushed and shot in the district on 3 March 1920.

Much of the chancel, admired by Dr. Pococke, was still standing in the eighteenth century but today only the piers and their columns remain for admiration. The capitals are decorated with intricate and varied 'scallop' work in Romanesque style. They, like the double light window of the central gable, are made of limestone which is much lighter than the rest of the building. The windows are narrow and semi-circular at the top and they are very like those at Clonfert and Clonmacnoise but are of better quality. One particular feature of Irish Romanesque to be seen in the O'Heynes monastery is the character of the quoins (wedged stones used at the angles of buildings). Here, as at Clonfert and at Teampul na Hue, the quoins are gracefully carved. Their presence is attributed to Maurice Illeyan, who was Bishop of Kilmacduagh in the thirteenth century. From the chancel on the south side, a doorway leads into the sacristy and into a room which may have been the monastery's treasury. A larger, nearby room may have been the dining room or refectory. Throughout, the vaulting is interesting.

The Leaning Tower

The most conspicuous structure at Kilmacduagh is its tall leaning tower rising high above the ruins. The door to the tower is actually 26 feet up from ground level presumably so that in times of danger the monks could climb ladders, pass safely inside and pull the ladder in after them. Attackers would have found it impossible to get at the holy men within. According to Robert Cochrane, in an article to the Royal Society of Antiquaries in 1904, the tower measures 94 feet 10 inches [28.8m] from the ground to the base of the conical cap which is itself 17 feet [5.16m] high. In all then the tower is just a couple of inches short of 112 feet [33.9m] high; probably the tallest in Ireland.

The Board of Works made considerable repairs to the tower in 1879. Crumbling masonry was removed and the capping was made safe. The installation of a lightning conductor led to the removal of debris built up slowly but inexorably there over the centuries, inside the old tower. From the door sill downwards the debris consisted of: two feet of twigs and debris of birds; 4 feet [1.2m] of fallen stone and rubbish; 3 feet [0.9m] of decomposed twigs and small bones; 3 feet [0.9m] of brown earth, ashes and small bones; 9 feet 10 inches [3m] of ashes and oyster shells, in which pieces of copper were found; 6 feet 2 inches [1.86m] of small stones. Beneath all this, lay human bones and skeletons, the remains of an ancient burial ground. (Robert Cochrane, *Notes on the Round Tower of Kilmacduagh*, Royal Society of Antiquaries, 1904).

The tower itself was built upon a very slight foundation possibly over an ancient burial ground. At door level, the walls are 4 feet 6 inches [1.37m] thick and at ground level 6 feet 6 inches [1.98m] thick. The only footings were one foot high and 20 inches [0.51m] out from the edge of the tower! Beneath those was soft earth. The massive structure leans two feet out of perpendicular but is not in any danger of collapse!

In ancient times, the monastery stood between two loughs which were said to evacuate themselves in the summer into whirlpools; a distinct possibility considering the cavernous nature of the ground in the whole district.

According to tradition the tower at Kilmacduagh had bells which were flung into the waters of a small lake, one of the loughs. According to Fahey, a peasant in the nineteenth century knew exactly where the bells lay but the owners of the nearby property could not agree to recover them.

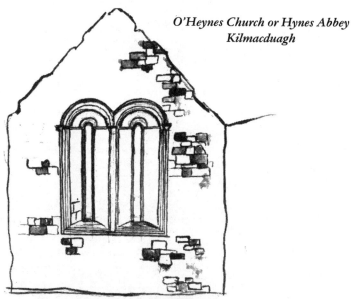

O'Heynes Church or Hynes Abbey
Kilmacduagh

Irish Romanesque double light window

Decorated capitals
chancel arch

The ancient bells lie there still, not far from the tower. It is likely that the churches were still in use in the mid-seventeenth century but after Bishop Hugh de Burgo's exile in 1656, the abandonment of the site led to an eventual long-term neglect.

Although, long ago, the churches in Kilmacduagh were restored after the depredations of the Norse raiders, the holy places were plundered during the thirteenth century when Irish and Norman on the one side fought Norman and Irish on the other. The shame of it was that it was Christian men who then wrought the havoc.

The abbey was probably wrecked in the beginning of the 13th Century by William Fitz Adelm de Burgo to revenge his defeat at Kilmacduagh at the hands of Cathal the Red-handed O'Connor but it was rebuilt later by the Augustinian Canons. The rivalry of the O'Connor princes led to a battle in the forests surrounding the monastery in the year 1200 AD. Cathal Carrach and William FitzAdelm de Burgo fought Cathal of the Red Right Hand supported by De Courcy. After that battle, Cathal Carrach and de Burgo, "Left neither church nor territory from Echtghe to Dun Rossarach and from Sinuum westward to the sea, nor canon, nor abbot, nor bishop was afforded protection against the demoniacal host." So say the 'Annals of Lough Ce.

A second raid that year, by the same army, devastated Connaught when almost all the churches there were burned. Then in 1201, Crovedaearg returned with De Courcey, De Lacy and a 'great number of foreigners (Normans)" to be defeated once more at Kilmacduagh where sixty nobles of the De Courcey's followers were slain.

Yet again, in 1204, William de Burgo plundered the churches of Connaught including those of the Ui Fiachrach Aidhne. Three years later, in 1207, Murtagh, son of Turlogh Mor O'Brien, plundered the churches of the district from Kilmacduagh to Athenry. Once more in 1225, Murtagh, son of Donal O'Brien, plundered and slaughtered throughout the area so that"There was not a church in Connaught on that day without being destroyed".

For Christians living in this present century, this raiding and plundering churches and monasteries by Christian warriors and their clergy is, to say the least, quite bewildering but there is documentary evidence not only for such raids but also for inter-monastery wars when abbots took up arms along with their provincial overlords and high kings! Furthermore and regrettably, warmongering clerics and the participation of monastic populations in military escapades happened not only in early historic Ireland but among clerics at all levels of the church hierarchy across Europe. The interdependence of church and tribe or state made going to war, one faction against another, seem inevitable. The famous Horses of St. Mark prancing on the front of the church of that name in Venice, looted in 1204 by Doge Enrico Dandolo from Constantinople illustrates the fact that clergy were not necessarily averse to receiving stolen goods!

Old habits die hard and in pre-Christian Ireland, over millennia, ritual 'hosting' took place wherein the conflicts among the gods were re-enacted by mortals. Warfare was a kind of religious obligation in pagan times and thus, unfortunately, it continued under the new religion. Warfare, like, speech, appears to be ingrained, in the human DNA!

After the restorations which followed that period of strife, during the Protestant Reformation, the church lands at Kilmacduagh were confiscated and conferred upon Richard, the second Earl of Clanricarde but he did not take them up. It is unlikely that any of the churches at Kilmacduagh were dismantled at that time because throughout the Gaelic areas, the reformers had little success and many grants of monastic land to Catholic grantees were left untouched. Connaught remained staunchly Catholic after the Elizabethan period and faithful to the old religion.

In his old age, St. Colman founded monasteries Teampuill "Temple" Mor Mhic Duagh and Teampuill beg Mhic Duagh on the Aran Islands. They are close to each other forming part of the famous group of Churches at Kilmurvy, known as The Seven Churches. There it is said St. Enda, whose monastery is close by, instructed St. Colman in the way of virtue. The island can be reached today by taking a high-speed ferry from Doolin.

At Corcomroe, four and a half miles east of Ballyvaughan, there is an abbey founded by Donal Mor O'Brien, built on the site of the original monastic foundation. The grey aspect of this Cistercian Abbey blends in with the colour of the karstic limestone hills of the Burren. In the graveyard there is a huge nineteenth century tomb of James Hynes and a mausoleum with a modern door inscribed with the name, HYNES. Southeast of Corcomroe, high up towards Turlough Hill lie the ruins another monastery founded by St. Colman, the church of Oughtmama. The saint, in fact, died there but was later buried at Kilmacduagh. W.B. Yeat's play 'The Dreaming of the Bones' is set there.

Guaire, His Brother Saint Caimin and Others

Among the stories relating to the life of Guaire are those associated with the king's half brother, Saint Caimin of Innis Cealtra and with Cummene Fota of Clonfert and also with Mac da Cherda (Son of two trades). *The Annals of the Four Masters* mention, "Cummianea, daughter of Delbronius, was mother of Caimin and Guaire" but they must have had different fathers. Cummianea is said to have been the progenitor of some seventy-seven saints of Ireland. It is possible that Guaire's reputation for generosity has been enhanced because of his patronage of these holy men, some of whom were Munster men living among the hermits of the Shannon. Caimin was Bishop Abbot of Inis Cealtra and possibly the first Bishop of Killaloe. The Annals of Inisfallen report that he died in 654.

Guaire's political and social influence extended into some regions of Munster which lay on the edge of the Ui Fiachrach's ecclesiastical district. Cummene Fota had influence in Clonfert and in Corcomruad. Saint Caimin had the same mother as Guaire so Guaire's friendship with him was very close. Both brothers were associated with the foundation of the monastery at Mountshannon, County Clare and with the foundation of the monastery on Inis Cealtra in Lough Derg.The Mountshannon ruins are situated on the Clare side of Lough Derg on the road from Portumna and they are the finest in the country. That monastery, too, in its time suffered from the depredations of Vikings but they too were restored under the patronage of Brian Borumna. On the site are the ruins of St. Bridget's, and St. Caimin's churches. There is a 'confessional', a round tower, two high crosses and an early cemetery. Many holy men settled there and on the islands and shores of Lough Derg.

Guaire is also associated with Tuamgraney Church which with St. Caimin's Church of Innis Cealtra were later looked after by the O'Briens, the Dalcassians who became the leading family in succession to the Aidhne In fact, the buildings at Tuamgraney (Tomb of Gráinne) were constructed by Cormac O'Killeen, d. 663 of the Ui Fiachrach Aidhne under the patronage of Brian Boru. [Tuamgraney is the birthplace of the Irish novelist, Edna O'Brien.]

INNIS CEALTRA

The island of Innis Cealtra, also known as Holy Island and as Church Island, is the second largest one in Lough Derg. It is unique in Western Europe in that it is an island burial place on which there are intact graves dating back to the eighth century with many of the original memorial stones in good condition. Although Guaire's brother founded the community there, other solitary hermits had inhabited the place before him. There, may be found, the dwelling of Cosrach the Miserable, who, for fear of hell, lived with "...a stone at his back, a stone on either side of him and a stone at his front." He died there in the year 898 and he even has a stone today, a headstone marker! He lived in the tiny corner of a hermitage he had built around an ancient cromlech, in a place where pilgrims had the most uncomfortable time trying to reach him for advice. The island is associated with a charming legend concerning Guaire and the two saints Caimin and Cummene Fota. The three men had met in Saint Caimin's Church when Caimin asked the others what they would like to see in abundance in the church. Guaire answered that he would like to see an abundance of gold and silver so that he might give it away to the poor. Cummene Fota wanted to see plenty of books to instruct his students and to spread the Word of God; while St. Caimin wanted the church to be filled with sickness and disease so that he might suffer it all on behalf of the rest of mankind!

All the wishes came true, in that, Guaire had the gold which he gave to the needy, Cummene gained wisdom and scholarship and Caimin suffered! Each man came in time to epitomise in turn - generosity, learning and penitential spirit. For many years patients were carried to Inis Cealtra in the hope of leaving their afflictions with the good man Caimin!

Saint Caimin also gained a reputation for literary merit. The 'Commentary on the Psalms' – a fragment of which is held by the Franciscans of Merchant's Quay in Dublin, has been attributed to him although the present fragment is probably thirteenth century.

Guaire has been described as a pious king. At one time, when Saint Fechin of the O'Hara family, and his priests were converting the people of the island of Immuagh and possibly High Island and Omey Island lying off the western coast. Guaire saved the lives of the islanders by sending an ample supply of provisions at the request of the missionaries. He was so well loved by these holy men of the Shannon that on one occasion as St. Madoc of the Fens was travelling to Cashel, he broke his journey on hearing that King Guaire was seriously ill. He then made his way, in haste, to the king's bedside at Dun Guaire where he prayed successfully for his recovery.

Among the seventy or more saints of the Ui Fiachrach lineage there are two, brother and sister, worthy of mention in this short history. They were Saints Foila and Colga, daughter and son of Aedh (Fire) Draicnighe, great grandson of Dathy. St. Foila was patroness of the Church of Kileely or Kilfoila in the Parish of Clarinbridge, just south of Galway. She was attributed with many miracles in her lifetime and many more afterwards. Her tomb was visited by many thousands of pilgrims until it fell to ruins and the pilgrimages were forgotten. Her shrine is a neglected ruin situated about half a mile from Kilcolgan and one and a half miles from the church of Dromacoo.

Actually the name of the town Kilcolgan is derived from Colga, son of Aid Draigniche, one of the grandsons of Fechrech and brother of Foila and Aidus and a disciple of the famous Saint Columba under whom he studied at Iona, Scotland during the sixth century. One night when on that beautiful Scottish island, while most of the brothers were asleep, Colga, stood near the church entrance, praying when he saw the whole church suddenly filled with a heavenly light, flashing like cosmic lightning. At the time he was unaware that Saint Columba was at prayer within at that very time. Alarmed he at once ran back to his own cell. The next morning Columba drew him to one side rebuking him saying, "Take care of one thing, my child, that you do not attempt to spy out and pry too closely into the nature of that heavenly light which was not granted thee, but rather fled from thee, and that thou do not tell any one during my lifetime what thou hast seen." But someone did tell. Who!

Before completing his studies Colga was advised to go back to Ireland to persuade his own mother, Cuilein, to repent of a sin committed in her youth with King Failbe Flann at Cashel. In the course of time Colga became abbot of the monastery at Kilcolgan where he died in the sixth century as Columba had foretold when Colga saw his brother making merry and turning the ladle in the soup!

Today it is difficult to place the site of Colga's monastery and church but in 1893 it was thought to have been on the site of a ruined Protestant Church in the grounds of Christopher St. George of Tyrone who was converted by Father Edward Heynes in the eighteenth century. The site could be half a mile south of the village of Kilcolgan near the castle

Saint Sairnait (Sourney) was yet another saint of the race of Eoghan Aidhne. Several wells in the district are dedicated to her. There is one at Dromacoo near Ballinderreen (little oakwood), some three and a half miles from Kinvara on the road to Kilcolgan where there is a stone cell measuring about six feet by four in which she lived. Within the old church nearby was a mausoleum for the Killikellys who occupied the neighbouring castle of Cloghballymore. In 1232 AD a hospital stood near there bearing her name. There is also a church, called Teampall Asurnaí dedicated to her on the Aran Isles. East of the church, a small rectangular building, St. Sourney's Bed, may be her burial place. The associated Sourney's Hermitage is located near the village of Eochaill in the central part of Inishmore in the area known as Mainstir off either the coast road or the upper road.

Guaire's Successors

Guaire's overlordship extended into Thomond and Corcomruad and Corco Baiscinn. The failure of the Aidhne to retain control of those territories seriously weakened their position and left the way open for the eventual successes of the Ui Briuin. After Guaire's defeat by the High King and his allies, Maenach, son of Baithin, king of the Ui Briuin defeated Guaire's ally, Marcan mac Tommáin, a son-in-law married to Creide, who was killed in battle in Airthir Seola, in 653 by the Ui Briun princes Cenn Faelad mac Colgan and Máenach mac Báethíne. At the time Guaire's brother, Loingsech mac Colmain held the kingship. He had been king of the Ui Maine, [think O'Kelly] and a son-in-law of Guaire's at the time when his wife Creide had a love affair with Cano. The Uí Maine were allies and subjects of the Ui Fiachrach Aidhne under Guaire's rule. Then in 654 AD, Guaire killed Muirgius together with his allies Fergus and Aedh (Fire). But, as there was no strong successor to Guaire from the Ui Fiachrach Aidhne after Guaire's death in 663, the Ui Briuin power grew stronger while Aidhne power weakened. The Ui Maine link of O'Kelly allegiance loosened and the two kingdoms fought each other in 743.

MacFirbis refers to: "...the four kings of the province of Connaght who dwelt in Aidhne, land of saints, Muircheartach (one of the perfect breed), Laighen, Guaire and Colman Caomb".

Guaire had other royal residences in addition to the one at Kinvara; one in Gort Inse Guaire {The tilled field on the island of Guaire} and another near the River Moy. Nothing remains of them today and nothing remains of the O'Shaughnessy Castle in Gort which took the place of the old fort. In later times, a military barracks for British soldiers was built out of the stones but that too has now gone although the remains of one wall and window may still be distinguished.

When close to death Guaire, the Hospitable, went on pilgrimage to Clonmacnoise to do penance for his sins and died there in 663 to be buried with great honour. Even after death his honour lived on in a practical way for it is said that a jester made a pilgrimage to the good king's grave and on kneeling to ask for a favour was rewarded as the king's hand reached out of the earth to pour a handful of dust beside the appellant. The dust turned to gold as it fell! The Annals of Innisfallen mention a battle in the year 665 in which the Connachta fought the Munstermen at Loch Fén (Loughfane, County Limerick) but there was no mention of winners or losers or whether the Connachta fought or it was only the Ui Fiachrach Aidhne. According to several annals, Guaire's son, Celach mac Guairi also died during a plague in 666, shortly after his father

Clonmacnoise

Among Guaire's sons was Muirchertach Nár mac Guairi progenitor of the O'Moghans. He too died shortly after his father in 668 after possibly holding the Kingship of Connacht for a few years. However, The Book of Leinster, does not show Muirchertach Nár mac Guairi as king whereas the Chronicum Scotorum of the Irish annals does, naming him as king of Connacht in his death obit. Unfortunately too, Guaire's grandson Airmedach met with violent death in 675. The murderous struggles for power among neighbouring tribes continued such is the way of people, Christian or not!

Another successor to the kingship of Connaught was Cennfáelad mac Colgan son of Colgu of the Uir Briuin although he was killed shortly afterwards in 682 by the Ui Fiachrach Aidhne.

In 683, Dunchad of the northern Ui Fiachrach, was slain by the southern Aidhne, possibly by Fergus Aidhne, son of Artgal who then became the seventeenth King of Connaught. He died in the year 696 after what was thought to be a fairly peaceful reign. Fergal was succeeded by Muiredach Muilleithan, son of Murgius who was killed by the Ui Fiachrach Aidhne in 654 despite his having been married to Guaire's daughter Creide after the death of her previous husband Marcan son of Tomain. (See story of Cano and Creide for a different version).

Yet another of Guaire's sons, Arthgal mac Guairi, himself had two sons, Aodh, (Cenel nAeda) ancestor of the O'Shaughnessys and Artgoil, ancestor of the O'Heynes, O'Clearys and MacGillakellys (Killikellys; sometimes shortened to Kellys. R.J. Kelly, the historian, maintains that the Ui Briuins, who came to monopolise the kingship of Connaught were collateral branches of Arthgal's descendants known later as O'Flahertys and O'Connors and therefore related to Guaire's direct descendants.

By the year 707, the Ui Briuin were well on their way to increased power with their representative Indrechtach mac Muiredaig holding the kingship of Connaught. During his reign some of the minor tribes moved their allegiance from the Ui Fiachrach Aidhne to the Ui Briuins.

In 782, during the reign of Tipraite mac Taidg, King of Connaught, who died in 786, severe attacks were launched upon both the Ui Fiachrach Aidhne and the Ui Fiachrach of the north. The Aidhne had to fight once again on their traditional battleground of Carn Conaill, near Gort, where in 784 Tipraite defeated them. He fought and defeated the northern branch of the Ui Fiachrach Aidhne the next year, at the Battle of Muad (Moy River). The Ui Briun gained the kingship of Connacht.

Several years later in 787, the Aidhne made brave attempts to regain some of their lost power by winning two battles in the first of which they killed Dub Dibeirgg mac Cathail of the Ui Briuin but lost their own King, Cathmug mac Duinn Cothaid in the fight. In the second battle, the new leader of the Ui Briuin, Umaill, was slain but no long term advantage was gained by the Aidhne as the eighth century came to an end.

The traditional allies of the Ui Fiachrach, the Ui Maine (Kellys) extended their influence into Roscommon and south-east Galway but after the 12th Century they were confined to Clonfert while the O'Hynes exercised their influence within the bounds of the diocese of Kilmacduagh. Although the Ui Fiachrach, the Ui Briuin and the Ui Ailella were known as the Three Connachta, by the time the Danes were settling in Ireland the Ui Briuin were regularly providing the kings of Connaught. Some three hundred and fifty years after the death of Guaire, the O'Hynes, the O'Kellys and the O'Briens joined forces to drive the Vikings out of Ireland and subdue rivals to the High Kingship at the Battle of Clontarf.

The Battle of Clontarf
THE VIKING TERROR

Bitter is the wind tonight
It tosses the ocean's hair
Tonight I fear not the fierce warriors of Norway
Coursing on the Irish Sea
From Kuno Meyer's Ancient Irish Poetry

The Norse attacks upon Ireland in 795 began with their landing at Lambay Island. Although Ireland had been spared invasion by the Romans during the 8th Century, the wild men sallying forth from a wild country, Norway sought new lands and opportunities. They sailed in superb boats with superb weapons as economic migrants with attitude, attacking and gaining footholds in several important regions: Dublin, Waterford and Limerick where they settled with families and set up trading posts. Not unexpectedly many of the Irish welcomed the prosperity from the lucrative trading posts which they were able to share with the foreigners who were now their new neighbours integrated with the local population. On the other hand, the attacks by the Norsemen on the Irish monasteries were very damaging as of course were Irish raids on the monasteries located in their tribal enemy's territories. Irishmen attacking and looting churches and monasteries themselves was one thing but allowing foreigners to do it was quite another!

During the ninth century the Danes raided places on the west coast of Ireland, in Connaught for example, but although the Norsemen destroyed many ancient documents, the scholarship and learning for which the Irish were noted continued to flourish. Aidhne scholars continued with their exercises in learning. For example, the death, in 806, of a scholarly descendant of Guaire, Connmhach, a scribe from the monastery of Clonmacnoise, was recorded in The Four Masters. Another such, one of the greatest of poets for centuries was the great Flan Mac Lonan O'Guaire who died in the year 896 AD after gaining an outstanding reputation during his own lifetime.

Despite their great longships, all was never plain sailing for the Danes, certainly not on land. Wolves of the sea they may have been but they had fierce competition from wolves of the land, the Irish warriors. In his elegy on the death of the son of Dalach, an ancestor of the O'Dalys, MacLonan describes the slaughter of many Danes by the Tirconnellians who had been forced to pay tribute for some years to the "Danish pirates".

The Danes attacked Kinvara in 866 during their raids on various monasteries in the West of Ireland including Kilmacduagh where no doubt the monks took refuge in the round tower which must, nevertheless, have been an obvious landmark for the raiders. In 920, Maol mac Duach, Lord of Aidhne, was killed by the Danes while defending his territories. Some years later, in 938, Harold, grandson of Sitric, Lord of the Danes of Limerick, was killed by the Caenrighe in the Aidhne territory, within the present townland* of "Raheen," (Ratheyney) in the parish of Ardrahan. That death was just a few years before the great scourge of the Danes, Brian Boru was born and by 960, Brian, a member of the Dalcassians, the O'Briens, along with other young adventurers including young princes of Aidhne, waged a successful guerrilla war on the Norsemen. Brian's successes, first against small bands of half a dozen or so Danes at a time, drew young Irish warriors to his side in increasing numbers and although these warriors lived rough, their numbers grew into a formidable army.

*A townland is one of the smallest land divisions in Ireland. They range in size from a few acres to thousands of acres. Many are Gaelic in origin, but some came into existence after the Norman invasion of 1169.

After the Dalcassians had seized the Munster throne, in 964, Brian was crowned King of Munster and then in 1002 Brian ousted Malachy II from the High Kingship of Ireland and assumed the position himself. That move was not at all popular with the Leinster men who actually allied themselves with powerful Norse chieftains against Brian and some of his Norse supporters. However, after the battle of Glenaama in Wicklow, the King of Leinster and the Danes of Dublin were routed and after following an all too brief policy of reconciliation Brian married Gormflaith the mother of Sitric, the Danish King of Dublin. Sitric in his turn married Brian's daughter whose mother was Mor O'Heyne, an earlier wife of

* A townland is one the smallest land divisions in Ireland. They range in size from a few acres to thousands of acres. Many are Gaelic in origin, but some came into existence after the Norman invasion of 1169.

Brian. Thereafter Brian exacted 150 vats of wine from the Dublin Danes as tribute, and a daily barrel of wine from the Limerick Vikings.

During the short period of Brian's hegemony he sponsored restoration of buildings destroyed by the Norsemen. He built bridges, increased his naval forces and encouraged centres of learning in much the same way as King Alfred of the West Saxons had done in England. His own hill fort on the banks of the Shannon at Kincora, once a target of the Limerick Danes was reinforced.

Brian had many sons, the oldest ones to his first wife Mór ingen Eiden, Mor O'Heyne, possibly the daughter of Flann Eidhin, son of Cleireach who was ancestor of the O'Clerys. One authority places Mor as daughter of Mulroy O'Heyne. Three of her sons, Morogh, Conchobar and Flann were killed in the vicious Battle of Clontarf. Morogh, son of Brian Boru and Mor O'Heyne, distinguished himself while still a boy in 978 when he slew the chief of the Ui Fidghenti, Hy Fighenty, located in today's County Limerick, in hand to hand combat during a battle which brought Brian the Kingship of Munster. [Ui Fidghenti lived in the home territory of the MacClerkens and O'Clerkins, now anglicised as Cleary and Clarke.]

The conflict between Brian and some of the Danes on the one side and the Norse with some of their Irish allies on the other side, came to a bloody conclusion at the Battle of Clontarf when Brian's challenger, Mael Morda, King of Leinster and his Norse allies, fought a vicious battle under the walls of Dublin. Gormflaith, sister of the King of Leinster, and wife or mistress to three successive kings, one of them Brian himself, had been repudiated, rejected, by Brian, so, she actively engaged in helping Mael Morda to gather the forces aligned against Brian. Her son, Sitric, promised Brodar of Man, Admiral of the Danish fleet, and Sigurd of the Orkneys, separately, the title of King of Ireland and the hand of his mother in marriage if their attack proved successful. (A marriage of convenience if ever there was one as Gormflaith must have been exceedingly old by then!).

In the immediate months before the Battle of Clontarf, another of Brian's sons, Donogh, was actively engaged in plundering Leinster so Brian's opponents sought battle near Dublin before Donogh could return to help his father. Mael Morda and his Norsemen allies despatched messengers to Danish strongholds and colonies to bring in large reinforcements and the Bay of Dublin filled with long ships from Norway, Denmark, Orkney, Shetland, Man, Skye, Lewis, Northumbria, Cantire, Cornwall, Iceland, the Hebrides and Normandy. The King of Denmark's sons, Carolus, Kanutus and Andreas headed 12,000 men. Brodar and Anrad led 1000 handpicked troops clad from head to foot in mail. Along with them were the Irishman Mael Morda and his Leinster men together with Flaherty O'Neill of Tirowen and O'Rorke of Breffni who had been contesting with Brian's ally Malachy. In all, Brian's opponents were said to have amounted to over 20,000 warriors. That is probably an exaggerated figure. One could hardly have found room for them all on the field of battle!

Brian's five sons, at least one grandson, fifteen nephews, and the whole contingent of Dalcassion warriors together with all the chiefs of North Munster gathered together to do battle along with the chieftains and men from South Munster and the forces from Connaught and Meath.

The Dalcassians from Brian's home territory were led by the O'Briens, O'Deas, MacNamaras and the O'Quinns whose warriors claimed the privilege of being first in the battle and last out! The fighting men from Ormond across the Shannon arrived, the Hy Fidgenti, the forces of Desmond, the Deisi under their chief Mothla. The Connaught forces were led by Mulrony O'Heyne, Teige O'Kelly and O'Flaherty of West Connaught. The Great Stewards of Scotland, of Lennox and of Marr and many other Scottish-Scandinavian chieftains joined Brian against their own kinsmen. Notions of nationhood really didn't enter into it but rather self-interest ruled the day. Brian entertained ideas of a united Ireland so long as he was head of it but his traditional enemies rejected that ambition out of hand.

Scandinavian sagas mention the signs and omens observed by the warriors in the weeks leading up to the conflict. They tell of Brodir seeing a shower of blood fall from the sky; of birds in conflict in the air; of swords and spears wielded by invisible arms among the clouds. In Iceland, it was said, a priest, saying mass, had his vestments splashed with blood (By then some of the Vikings had taken up Christianity!) and in Caithness, Scotland, warriors saw Valkyries weaving horrible patterns with shuttles which moved through men's entrails! They were of course reading the shapes in the aurora borealis in northern skies when billions of electrons stream towards the Earth along its magnetic fields, colliding with air particles. Brian, too, was visited by the family banshee, which told him that he would not survive the ensuing battle while Brodar, his enemy claimed that he had an omen telling him to insist upon battle on the Good Friday for then the victory would go to the Danes. Brodar's omen no doubt had something to do with fact that he had been a practising Christian, in fact a mass deacon, until he gave it up and returned to the old gods. Brian's forces encamped before the battle near Phibsborough in Tomar's Wood, on high ground, while the enemy camped closer to the shore by Tolka and Clontarf.

The Battle did indeed begin on a day Brian would have wished to avoid because of its holiness, but the enemy after having been invited, as was the custom, to choose the time and place, insisted upon the morning of Good Friday, 23 April, 1014. In the dawn light, before the fighting began, Brian mounted upon a battle charger, rode with his son, Morogh, holding a crucifix in his left hand and his sword in his right, between the ranks of his army and is supposed to have addressed them with:

"Be not dismayed because that my son Donogh, with the third part of the Momonian forces is absent from you, for they are plundering Leinster and the Danish territories. Long have the men of Ireland groaned under the tyranny of the seafaring pirates! Murderers of your kings and chieftains, plunderers of your fortresses! Profane destroyers of the churches and monasteries of God! Who have trampled upon and committed to flames the relics of his saints! May the Almighty God, through his great mercy, give you strength and courage this day, to put an end forever to the Lochlunian tyranny in Ireland, and to revenge upon them their many perfidies and their profanities of the sacred edifices dedicated to his worship, this day on which Jesus Christ himself suffered death for your redemption".

The prebattle speech is of course is mostly speculation but the gist of it is there because the poets and chroniclers, the journalists of the time, would have been present right throughout the day to remember and record the deeds of the leading chieftains. Brian then made his way to the centre of his troops to lead them to battle but because of his great age he was persuaded to leave operational command to Morogh and for him to exercise overall command from a tent, in safety, away from the field of conflict.

The battle then began, it is said, when the Danish champion Plat challenged an Irish champion to single combat with a challenge: "Where is Donal?" Upon hearing this, the Great Steward of Marr, Donal, a heroic supporter of Brian, answered: "I am here, Reptile!" And with that both warriors fell upon each other and within minutes killed each other in fierce and bloody solitary combat as befitted two warriors of high reputation.

The main battle followed on that early Good Friday morning with a series of single hand-to-hand engagements where personal prowess counted for so much as did the honour of the top champions who sought out fitting opponents to fell with sword and axe. Each tribesman gathered around his chief who tried to single out warriors of similar rank worthy of his attentions. The victors of one fight in their turn became the victims of fresh opponents as the day wore on and the fighters grew tired and faint from their wounds and bruises.

Clontarf, 1014 A.D.

It was a battle of mixed loyalties as the Norse army supported by Irish fought the Irish army supported by some Danes! Many of the Dublin Danes fought alongside Brian while others stayed away from the battle in the town. The main battle raged very close to the city but moved during the course of the day out towards Howth and Conquer Hill where the final issue was decided near where the Clontarf Yacht Club now stands. The battle was so fierce that the opposing forces came close to exterminating each other completely.

Very early in the battle, Maelscachlainn,(Malachy), the King of the Meath treacherously took his men off the field to watch the conflict from a nearby meadow leaving Brian's forces seriously depleted. On seeing the action Morogh, Brian's son and battle commender, called out to his Dalcassians urging them to take heart because now they would have all the more glory in defeating the enemy without the traitors' aid. In this first division of Brian's forces were four more of his sons: Teige, Donald, Connor and Flann. Morogh's son, Turlough grandson of the O'Heyne, a boy of fifteen fought as a warrior in his own right. He was slain and after the battle his body was from a sea weir with one arm entwined in the hair of his dead Viking opponent!

The Connaughtmen led by O'Heyne (Maolrunaiddh na Paidre that is Mulrony of the Prayer-so called because of his piety) and O'Kelly formed Brian's third division on the left as they faced the infamous Brodar and Loder, Earl of Orkney and the Viking adventurers from overseas. The O'Heyne warriors were said to have been adept at using an axe in each hand equally well. During the course of the day O'Heyne met his death and so too did Teige O'Kelly: "In the Battle of Brian, Teige fell as a wolf dog, pursuing the Danes". According to tradition the body of Teige Mor O'Kelly was recovered from the seashore after a fabulous beast, an enfield, had emerged from the ocean to stand guard over the dead body. (The enfield appears on the O'Kelly arms to this day as the family crest.)

During the day Morogh and his son Turlogh, flew from place to place leaving bloody bodies and limbs marking their advances. The success of Morogh so enraged Carolus and Conmael of Denmark that both attacked him at the same time, but despite that they both fell to Morogh's sword! During the day, Sitric, the Dane, and his men noticed that Morogh and other chiefs left the fighting now and then to immerse themselves in a cool well to quench their thirsts and to ease their hands swollen from holding battleaxe and sword. He successfully attacked the well with its twelve Irish guards to prevent the chiefs renewing their strengths there! However, his triumph was short lived for as soon as Sitric was back in the main battle Morogh singled him out and with one blow of his axe split him in two, through his armour.

Despite the heavy slaughter no advantage was gained either way until at about four o'clock in the afternoon the Irish made a fiercesome attack upon the enemy. The Danes began to give way as so many of the leaders singled out by the chiefs under Brian had been slain, their body parts strewn all over the shore. By this time Morogh's hands were swollen so badly that he could no longer lift his arm let alone wield a weapon.

In that condition he was attacked by Anrudh, son of Ebhric, but Morogh clutched his opponent with his left hand, shook him out of his protective mail and pinning him down, drove his sword through him by leaning his chest on the pommel and pressing with his body. The dying Anrudh plucked Morogh's own dagger from his enemy's belt and drove it into Morogh who died of the wound the next day after making his peace with God.

Following this incident, the Danes fled in all directions but some of those fleeing Danes led by Brodar came upon the seventy-three years old Brian kneeling before a crucifix in his tent. The first warning of danger was uttered by a servant who begged him to flee before the retreating Danes.

"Retreat becomes us not", said Brian. "I shall not leave this place alive for last night Aebhell of Cragla came to me and told me I should be killed this day. Take my horses to Armagh and communicate my will to the successor of St. Patrick. I bequeath my soul to God and my body to Armagh". He then outlined his plans for his interment. Such are the accounts of the annalists that Brian's actual words appear to have been reported but this is actually a conflation of two separate utterances for the sake of dramatic effect. (Cragla was a powerful, beautiful banshee)

"Green naked people are coming toward us", the alarmed servant cried. The green was probably an accurate description of oxidised bronze armour.

"They are Danes in armour", said Brian and so saying he seized his sword and went out to meet them.

According to one version, Brodar approached with some followers covered
entirely in armour. Brian swung a blow at Brodar cutting off the Dane's left
leg below the knee and his right foot from the ankle but Brodar's axe split
Brian's head and Brian was able to kill another attacker before dropping
dead himself. In another version Brodar kills Brian but is himself captured
then killed by disembowelment as he is tied to a tree and his intestines
wound around it!

Irish Warriors favoured axes

Malachy, who had refused to join Brian in the early morning, holding
his warriors in readiness in a nearby field led his fresh troops into battle
swinging their weapons around their heads on the winning side and lived to
regain the High Kingship after Brian's death. After the battle he described

his experiences while holding his men out of the conflict when he said:"We retired to the distance of a fallow field from the combatants, the high wind of the Spring blowing from them to us. And we were no longer than half an hour there when neither of the two armies could discern each other, nor could one know his father or brother, even though he were the next to him, unless he could recognise his voice, or know that spot on which he stood, and we were covered all over, both faces, arms, heads, hair and clothes with red drops of blood, borne from them on the wings of the wind".

Of some of the divisions of Norsemen not one was left alive. The thousand or so in mail were all cut to pieces! An historian, O'Donovan, wrote that "... very few of the O'Kellys or the O'Heynes survived it". The two clans lost so many that their political power went into serious decline. The O'Connors who had quarrelled with Brian and refused to join him in battle were able to succeed to the kingship of Connaught with little opposition from their old neighbouring tribes.

Giraldus Cambrensis writing in the time of the English King, John, described the havoc caused by the Irish warriors with their axes:"They hold the axe with one hand, not with both, the thumb being stretched along the handle and directing the blow: from which neither the helmet erected into a cone can defend the head, nor the iron mail the rest of the body. Whence it happens in our times that the whole thigh of a soldier, though ever so well cased in iron mail, is cut off by one blow of the axe, the thigh and left leg falling on one side of the horse, and the dying body on the other!"

It should be remembered that for many centuries still, after this battle that the Irish disdained the use of armour as unmanly and they fought clothed only in their linen tunics! Incidentally the scene of the battle brought the first mention of a name which later became famous in Irish history — that of Doyle. It was at Dubhgall's (Doyles, the black strangers) Bridge the crossing connecting the north side from the battlefield, that Tiege O'Kelly's men and Malachy's fresh Irish warriors, slew retreating Danes!

The Land of Glorious Aidhne

Let us approach Aidhne of the steeds
Their nobles and hospitality
Let us trace its kings who are not scarce
Let us touch the race of the nobles
Let us mention Aidhne — a duty without exception

Let us leave the tribes of Connaught
Let us sweetly sing their nobles
Let us mention the chiefs of Hy Fiachrach
The Mac Gillakellys, the pure
The O'Heyns of the beautiful slender steeds
Whose pride is defended by their arms
Of the race of Guaire of fair brows

Good the hero and festive
O'Clery, who is of their race (tribe)
Over the fair Kinel Kingawna
Rules O'Duibhghrolla who is of their country

Mag Fiachrach of famous name
Rules over the heavy haired youths of Beathra
Over Cinel Setna of rods
Rules O'Cahan, brave their battle
They possess the profits of the shore and flood
O'Moyna over the plain of Koenry

Two kings over Kind Aodha, the noble
O'Shaughnessy whom we do not avoid
And O'Cahill of the clergy
Smooth his fields and fertile mountain.

The Ui Fiachrach Aidhne furnished Connaught with several kings during the sixth and seventh centuries: Guaire Aidhne, the most famous of them. His reign marked the zenith of their power, for during the next 1000 years there was a steady decline in their political influence. From the 12th Century onwards the diocese of Kilmacduagh marked the boundaries of their power and even there they shared the territory with the O'Shaughnessys and the rest of their kinsmen.

During the 8th Century, the Ui Briuin made considerable gains in the province of Connaught and came in time to monopolise the Kingship of the province but during the Anglo-Norman period their place was taken by the O'Connors who had not participated in the Battle of Clontarf. So many eligible princes and chieftains of the O'Heyne and O'Shaughnessy were slain in 1014 that much of their power had been lost forever.

Immediately after the death of Brian, Malachy II once again took up the High Kingship of Ireland but he and his successors 'in opposition' as they were resisted by the many sub-kings. Between 1073 and 1084 AD, Turlough O'Brien, grandson of the great Brian held the title High King and his son, Murtough succeeded him in turn. Mulfavill O'Heyne, brother of Mulrony who was slain at Clontarf continued the Aidhne line and held the kingship of Ui Fiachrach after the death of Cugaela O'Clery in 1025. Mulfavill was king for 23 years and he died in the year 1048. His successor was his son, Cugaela who is mentioned in the Annals of the Four Masters as having slain Domhnall Ruadh O'Brien in the year 1055.

After him came Giolla na naomh ('...of the plunder') O'Heyne, who died in 1100 and was buried at Clonmacnoise. Next came Flann, son of Giolla and then Conchobar (Conor), son of Flann O'Heyne. Between 1118 and 1156, Turlough O'Connor ruled as King of Connaught. Inter tribal wars continued as these particular groups of people like so many others around the world carried out their favourite occupation of slaughter using an array of weapons such as those dredged up in 1844 from the Shannon fords. In one haul there were elfstones, i.e. stone arrowheads, along with swords, spearheads and battle-axes, all made of brass or iron, together with ornamental scabbards.

The O'Clerys, bearing one of the oldest surnames ever, lost their succession to the chieftainship of Ui FiachrachAidhne after the death of Brian O'Clery. O'Cleary is one of the oldest surnames ever. About 500 years later Mícheál Ó Cléirigh, Michael O'Clery (c. 1590-1643) became the chief chronicler of the Annals of the Four Masters.

1047 AD The Year of the Great Snow

'Great snow in this year (the like of which was never seen) from the festival of Mary until the festival of Patrick, so that it caused the destruction of cattle and wild animals, and the birds of the air, and the animals of the sea in general.'

Mulfabhaill Ua h Eidhin died.

Domnhaill Ruadh Ua Brian was slain by Ua h Eidhin, Lord of Ui Fiachrach Aidhne.It should be borne in mind that when it is recorded that one king or prince killed another, the actual killing may have been done by one of the clan warriors but the deed is attributed to the prince.

Eoghan O'Clery was forced by the Normans to leave his home territory. Many of his sept settled in what is now Donegal and Derry.

"An army led by Toirdhealbhach Ua Comchobhain and the Connaught people made an excursion into Desmond where they plundered territories and churches then went into Termon with their plunder of cattle and spoils of war. During that expedition Aedh Ua hEidhin, Lord of the Ui Fiachrach Aidhne was killed in Munster".

According to the Annals of the Four Masters, sub anno 1121:
'A hosting by Toirdhealbhach son of Ruaidhrí into Munster, and he burned Ciarraighe Luachra and went from there eastwards through Munster, and burned Ua Caoimh's house on the bank of the Abha Mhór, and his scouts came to Magh Ceithniuil and Druim Fínghin. On that day were killed Muireadhach Ua Flaithbheartaigh, king of Iarthar Connacht, and Aodh Ua hEidhin, king of Uí Fhiachrach Aidhne, to avenge the profanation of Mo-Chuda, although Toirdhealbhach made compensation for the plundering. An encampment by Toirdhealbhach son of Ruaidhrí at Magh Biorra during the winter, and he made a settlement between Clann Charthaigh and Síol Briain, and they both submitted to him.'

Two sons of Giolla Cheolaigh (Gillikelly) O'Heyne, himself the son of Aedh (Hugh) were slain by treachery near the mouth of the River Galway. Presumably treachery as used here may mean they were waylaid rather than slain in battle.

1133 AD

Turlogh O' Brien had laid siege to a Hynes fortification near Dunkellin levelling the fort and destroying a historic red beech tree under which the local kings were inaugurated.

Gilla Mo Choinni Ua Cathail, a descendant of Cathal mac Ógán, was slain by O'Shaughnessy this year. He was the only member of the Ó Cathail sept ever to rule Aidhne. The ua Cathail were rulers of Cenél Áeda na hEchtge until they were expelled by their Ó Seachnasaigh cousins in the 13th century. They settled in north County Galway and little was heard of them afterwards. Thereafter the O'Shaughnessys held the lordship.

The Gillikelly mentioned above and his son Aedh were killed during a battle between Connaught and the Northerners. His surviving son, Giolla na naomh continued the line.

O'Shaughnessy fell in the battle of Ardee with Kinel Aodh. Ardee, 'Atha Fherdia' means the Ford of Ferdia in County Louth.

1161 AD

Murtogh Mac Loughlin was King of Ireland but by 1166, Rory or Roderic O'Connor held that title. The Kings of Connaught, Leinster and Munster fought for supremacy and when Rory expelled Dermot MacMurrough, King of Leinster, the exiled king appealed to the Anglo-Normans for help in regaining his lands.

Dermot travelled to Aquitaine to enlist the aid of King Henry II of England. Before very long, a band of eminent Anglo-Norman adventurers landed in Ireland with many well armed soldiers. MacMurrough's daughter Aoife, married Richard de Clare, the 2nd Earl of Pembroke, a Cambro-Norman (Normans in Wales) lord, the famous Strongbow. A long period of Irish subjugation to foreign rule began.

Encouraged by the Pope who wanted to impose Roman rites and customs upon the Irish Church, King Henry himself landed in Ireland to confirm his sovereignty over the ambitious conquerors. The Papal Bull Laudabiliter, issued by Adrian IV, was used to legitimise this particular land grab: so much for the peace of God that passeth all understanding! . Much of Leinster along with Waterford, Wexford and Dublin were soon subdued and the submission of many of the Irish chieftains followed.

More of the O'Clearys, descendants of Guaire and close kinsmen of the O'Hynes were dispersed from Galway.

In his time Roderic O'Connor, Monarch of Ireland, lived in O'Heyne territory, near Lough Corrib. He had failed to push out the invaders and was subsequently forced to give up his claim to the High Kingship after a treaty with Henry II. Thereafter Roderic styled himself King of Connaught as a vassal of Henry of England.

The Annals record the death of Maurice O'Heyne at the hands of the Munster men. It is not clear who succeeded after the death of Muirgheas (Maurice) Ua hEidhin in 1180.

On an island near Boyle in Roscommon, the rock of Lough Key Castle, was struck by lightning killing Duvesa, daughter of O'Heyne and wife of Conor MacDermot. The name Lough Key, comes from the word 'ce', the druid of the legendary king of the Tuatha de Danann who drowned when the waters of the lake burst out of the earth. On this occasion, the Lord of Moyling was killed along with some 700 others during the ensuing fire and by drowning. Both Maurice and Duvesa were probably children of Aedh who was killed in 1153.

1195 AD

William de Burgh had conquered Connaught and many Irish chieftains were dispossessed. By the turn of the century, fierce conflicts took place in the forests of Kilmacduagh. An O'Heyne castle at Ardrahan was built about this time on the site of an ancient stronghold. As mentioned previously, the rival O'Connors clashed at Kilmacduagh. Cathal was defeated there but returned with large new forces while Carrach and de Burgo plundered churches, homes and lands in the district. Later raids laid waste the whole of Connaught and in this period there were rumours of starving people taking to cannibalism.

Maoeleachlain Riabach O'Shaughnessy was lord of half the territory of Kinel Aodh.

1199 AD

John de Courcy, with the English of Ulidia, and the son of Hugo De Lacy, with the English of Meath, marched to 'Kilmacduagh to assist Cathal Crovderg O'Conor. Cathal Carragh, accompanied by the Connacians, came, and gave them battle: and the English of Ulidia and Meath were defeated with such slaughter that, of their five battalions, only two survived; and these were pursued from the field of battle to Rindown on Lough Ree, in which place John was completely hemmed in. Many of his English were killed, and others were drowned; for they found no passage by which to escape, except by crossing the lake in boats.

The battles and skirmishes between the English and the Irish continued unabated as struggles for land, power and possessions underpinned the socioeconomic basis for living and flourishing in medieval Ireland. The Christian notion of loving your neighbour and your enemy really had no place among these peoples, Irish and Norman alike.

Crovedearg with de Courcey, de Lacy and others were again defeated and many nobles were slain. That year Conchobar (Conor) O'Heyne died. He was the son of Maurice.

The churches of Kilmacduagh were plundered by William de Burgo in a vengeance attack; so too were the other lands of the Ui Fiachrach. William had arrived in Ireland in 1185 and was appointed Governor of Limerick by King Henry.

1207 AD

In alliance with de Burgo, who had married an O'Brien princess, Murtagh, son of Turlogh Mor O'Brien, was taking his share of the plunder and killing all he met. All too often, self interest outweighed loyalty to neighbouring Irish chieftains!

1210 AD

King John of England landed in Ireland in an attempt to impose his kind of order in 'a land of strife'. He set up a government which was independent of the Irish lords so that English law prevailed.

1211 AD

The death of Cugaola O'Heyne was recorded.

"Donnchadh O'Heyne had his eyes put out by Aod, the son of Cathal Croibhearg O'Conor without the permission of O'Conor himself" Both of these O'Heyne were sons of Hugh O'Heyne slain in 1153. His branch of the family were deprived of succession to the kingship when Donnchadh was blinded as kings were required to be physically unblemished and in theory morally unblemished too.

1222 AD

Giolla Mochoine O'Cathail, lord of Kinel Aodh, East and West, was slain by   O'Shaughnessy. (This was the last occasion when an O'Cahill was chieftain of Kinel Aodh (Kinelea) thereafter the O'Shaughnessys held the lordship.)

1224 AD

Giolla na Naomb Crom O'Shaughnessy was lord of the western part of Kinel Aodh na Echtge.

In this year, Ardrahan, then a town of considerable importance, was the 'principal residence' of Eoghan (Owen) O Heyne, d. 1252, in this time, quite a conspicuous figure. He was the son of Giolla na naomh O'Heyne and one of the chiefs of Connaught who fought, along with the sons of Roderic O'Connor, against Hugh, son of Charles the Red-handed O'Connor who was helped by the Anglo-Normans. (See Ardrahan Castle). The year before this, Maelmure, the bishop of Ui Fiachrach Aidhne and of Cenel Aeda "rested in 'Christ"that is he died. Aed Meith Ua Neill invaded Connacht to assist Donn Óge Mag Oireachtaigh who had been deprived of his lands by King Aedh Ua Conchobair. The war resulted in Ua Conchobair being usurped by Aedh mac Ruaidri Ua Conchobair, whom Ó hEidhin supported.

This year, Fachtna Ar Allgarth, 'combarb' (priest) of Drumaroo and an official of the Ui Fiachrach Aidhne who kept a leper house and a guesthouse 'rested'. He had been a man of great learning and a benefactor of the area. Gillakelly O'Heyne was killed along with many others when he joined Hugh, son of Roderic, who had escaped from the English. During the battle, many of the warriors fought with whitened battle-axes as it was rumoured that a famous warrior had been slain by such an axe. People are just as superstitious today about all manner of things.

A Gilla Ceallaigh Ó hEidhin was killed in battle in the Tuathas fighting alongside Connor mac Aedh mac Ruaidhri, but his relationship to Owen is unclear. It was in 1232 that "The kingdom of Connaught was again given to Hugh, the son of Roderic", Owen's lord, and that de Burgh began building the castle of Galway.

By then, Richard de Burgh was temporarily out of favour with Henry and in that year McCarthy attacked Tralee while Felim O'Connor advanced into Westmeath, burning and plundering. Donough O'Brien had also turned against de Burgh and after joining Felim attacked Limerick, plundering O'Heynes in his own territory for having consistently assisted de Burgh.

A major expedition was led into Connacht by Richard Mór de Burgh. At Ardcarne, "the English held a private consultation, at the request of Owen O'Heyne, who wished to be revenged on the Momonians, and on Donough Cairbreach O'Brien." They determined to travel through Uí Maine and Máenmaige to enter Thomond in secrecy, where they "committed great depredations."The English forces were shadowed by King Felim Ua Conchobair, who, with the men of Munster, came to a pitched battle with the English, and fought manfully. But the English cavalry and infantry, who were clad in armour, finally overcame them. Many were slain on both sides, but the Momonians suffered most loss, through the imprudence of Donough Cairbreach. The Connacians then returned home, and on the next day O'Brien made peace with the English, and gave them hostages.

1235 AD

Ten years after helping the O'Connors against the English, Eoghan O'Heyne had joined Richard, son of William Burke on his famous expedition up and down the length of Connaught. Leading the feudal host were: Fitz-Maurice (Lord Deputy of Ireland); Hugo de Lacy (the Earl of Ulster); Walter Riddlesford (Chief Baron of Leinster); Lord John Cogan; the English of Munster and "all the roothes of Ireland". In pursuit of Felim O'Connor, they crossed the ford at Athlone and after setting fire to the town, they proceeded to Elphin, where they burned the great church. From there, they went to the monastery of Ath Dalaarg on the River Boyle on the day before Trinity Sunday.

Looters among the common soldiers broke into the sacristy and made off with vestments, chalices and other church furnishings. On hearing this, the English nobles sent back what they could recover from the soldiers and made restitution to the monastery for what they could not recover. The war host then went marauding in Creit, Glencar and to a tower at Glenfarn carrying their loot to the Lord Deputy's camp at Ardcarne. Then as now, it was acceptable for nobles and kings to steal whole nations and their treasures but common soldiers looting for their own gain was not approved…officially!

Eoghan O'Heyne met the English nobles and planned an attack with them upon the Momonians, especially upon Donnchadh Cairbreach O'Brien. All then returned through Hy Many and Moinmoy into Thomond plundering as they went.

Felim, the son of Cathal Croibhdearg O'Conor, watched the English pass out of his territories and he held a council of war to go to the aid of the Momonians. Fighting daily skirmishes with the English he then fought a pitched battle with them, but, the English troops clad in heavy armour and using both infantry and cavalry beat the Connacians and Momonians; killing many of the latter. The Connacians retreated to their homes, and

Donnchadh was forced to make peace; handing many hostages over to the English.

After the English had returned to Connaught, Aodh O'Flaherty made peace with them to protect his own territories from attack. Felim then took with him, to O'Donell Mor, all the cattle belonging to those who would help him. That is those from the territories of Conmaicne Mara and Conmaicne Cuile. Along with him went the son of Maghnus and Conchobar Ruadh, the son of Muircheartach O'Conor, after leaving the countryside desolate.

The English advanced to Dun Mugdord and sent messengers to Maghnus, son of Muircheartach Muimhneach but he refused them peace and hostages. The English then attacked the Sons of Roderic O'Conor, plundering Achill and carrying their spoils to Driuimni.

While all this was going on, Eoghan O'Heyne and Aodh O'Flaherty had their numerous forces carry boats from Lough Corrib, from Bunbonan to Iomaire on Lionain, some five miles, to meet the Lord Deputy at the Callow of Inisheany. Roderic O'Flaherty, in an account written for Sir William Petty wrote: "Imairc an Linian, anciently Linan Kinn Mara, is a long green spot of land by the sea of Coelshlyroe (Killary) whither the boats of Lough Orbsen were drawn by the forces of West Connaught and the Hy Fiachry Aidhne from Bonbona to the sea for five miles, anno 1235, to invade the sea islands there, upon an expedition into the Owles by Maurice Fitz-Gerald (fitz Maurice), Lord Justice of Ireland; Richard de Burgo, Lord of Connaught; Hugh de Lacy, Earl of Ulster; the Lord Riddlesford... in pursuit of O'Connors, belonging to Felim O'Connor, King of Connaught."

Maghnus attacked the English on the water close to the islands. The English broke off fighting but on returning to their camp, they found the boats which O'Flaherty and O'Heyne had brought overland. These boats were taken to a large beach near Maghnus who then landed on Inis Raithin sending some of his men to Inis Aonaigh. When the English saw Maghnus landing on the islands, they launched their boats in pursuit and attacked Maghnus and his followers with numerous well armed soldiers. All who could not escape in the boats with were slain. The English then carried off all the cattle from the islands in Clew Bay, taking with them the islanders themselves who would have died of starvation had they been left behind.

Many of the common people were killed by the attacking forces but the English were instructed by their commanders to do no killing on the Friday when they landed on the islands north of Umhall in honour of the crucifixion of Christ! The English then spread their attacks to include Luffertane, Ballsadare (attacking O'Donnell there), Curleius and Calah Puirt na Cairge on Lough Key, where Felim O'Connor's men resisted them.

After the Lord Deputy and the English had knelt in prayer at the monastery of the Blessed Trinity, they constructed a siege engine which they used to take the fortress on Lough Key from Felim's men and those of Cormac Mac Dermot.

The Connacians were left without food, clothing and cattle and without peace having set Irish against Irish in the wars. Felim was forced to make peace and the English left him with five cantreds of land bereft of cattle but free from tribute. Maurice Fitzgerald, holding Sligo, was rewarded by Richard de Burgh for his help in quelling the Irish chieftains, with land taken from the O'Heyne territory in the baronies of Dunkellin and Kiltartan in Galway. The grants were written in Latin thus: duo can trels terre de Ofecherath (Ui Fiachrach Aidhne) sicut Rothy O hethyn (Ruardhri O h Eidhin) ea .... tenuit salvo et in manu retento can tredo de Kenoloth (Cenel Aodha or O'Shaughnessy country).

The land was to be held for the service of four knights and a rent of 40 marks. This grant was made in 1235 A.D. and was witnessed by Hugh de Lacey and others.

Maurice Fitzgerald was also given a grant of free warren in Ardrahan and Kilcolgan together with the market and fair at Kilcolgan. Half the cantred of Ogeherhie was given to Eoghan O'Heyne but most of that was lost by the O'Heyne in 1252 A.D.

Richard de Burgh's principal manor was at Loughrea, in a castle he had built in 1236

1236 AD

Eoghan O'Heyne was opposing Felim O'Connor by assisting Brian, son of Turlogh O'Connor who had been set up by the English as King of the Irish of Connaught.

1240 AD

Hugh, son of Giolla na Naomb Crom O'Shaughnessy was slain by Conchobar, son of Aodh, son of Cathel Crovedearg O'Connor.

1247 AD

Conchobar O'Muiredag, who was bishop of Ui Fiachrach Aidhne, died in Bristol.

On May the 25th, Eoghan O'Heyne, in the presence of the Archbishop of Armagh, passed more land over to Fitzgerald from the cantred of Ogeherhie except for the 'feoffes' of Conor O'Heyne, Master Maurice, Thomas Malet and Nesta, daughter of Thomas, son of Robert. In return, Eoghan was granted the villata of Tillog and Punchedath in Ardrahan along with 8 cows and 40 marks of old Flemish money! Both O'Heyne and O'Shaughnessy had assisted Richard de Burgh for quite some time so they were not left landless as some chieftains had been by this time. Both O'Heyne and O'Shaughnessy kept most of their land but they were now officially subordinate

1253 AD

"Owen Ó hEidhin, Lord of Hy-Fiachrach Aidhne, died."

1258 AD

Kilcolgan was burned in struggles between the Sons of Roderic O'Connor and Cathal O'Connor.

1261 AD

Maelfabhaill or Mulfavill O'Heyne slew Hugh, son of Maolseachlainn O'Connor.

1263 AD

Mulfavill himself was killed by the English.

1264 AD
Ardrahan Castle was mentioned in the Annals of Lough Ce.

1264 AD

A castle at Lough Mask and the O'Heynes Castle at Ardrahan captured by Walter de Burgo. It was shortly after this that the O'Clerys were expelled from their lands in Aidhne.

1283 AD

The Canons Regular of St. Augustine were established at the Hynes Abbey at Kilmacduagh by Maurice Ileyan, Bishop.

1300 AD

By this year twelve shires modelled upon English lines had been established in Ireland, each of them under a royal sheriff. The Anglo-Nomians had consolidated their conquests and in the years to follow they became Irish themselves (e.g. de Burgh to Burke). The ultimate defeat of the pre-conquest Irish chieftains had been inevitable in the face of: the moral support given by the Pope to their conquerors; conquest in battle by large numbers of well armed forces and the traditional inability of Celtic peoples to unite solidly against a common enemy, preferring instead to settle old scores against each other.

John, the son of Eoghan O'Heyne, who had died in 1253, succeeded as chief of the name. Hugh, son of John, ruled next and his son Donogh succeeded him in turn.

1316 AD

Burke, Bermingham and the Anglo-Norman alliance inflicted a bloody defeat on Phelim O'Connor. At the end of the battle there were over 8000 dead on the field; most of them Irish chivalry.

1318 AD

The Scots, helping the Irish, were defeated near Dundalk and afterwards the Anglo-Norman hold was strengthened.

1326 AD

The death of Nicholas O'Heyne was recorded.

1340 AD

Eoghan, son of Donogh O'Heyne, Lord of the Ui Fiachrach Aidhne, was killed by his own followers, by his own kinsmen! (It is likely he was not a very pleasant man). The lordship passed to his brother, Muircheartach O'Heyne.

1377 AD

An army led by Richard Burke entered territory of the Clann Coilen who had assembled around MacNamara. MacNamara's forces inflicted a defeat upon the Clanrickard and in doing so slew Theobald, son of Ulick Burke, who was commanding a large body of Kerns (Irish foot soldiers armed with swords, wooden targes and bows). Three sons of O'Heyne were killed the same day in the battle.

1401 AD

Ulick Burke, son of Richard of Clanrickard, was drowned in Turloch Mor of the Ui Fiachrach Aidhne.

1403 AD

Muirehertach Garb O'Sechnusaig, an eligible prince of the Ui Fiachrach Aidhne, was killed by the Ui Maine (think of O'Kelly). O'Heyne fought alongside William Burke against Conor Roe at the Battle of Cillachaiah in Ui Maine, in the barony of Athlone, County Roscommon. Burke, Redmond MacHubert and O'Heyne were taken prisoner. (This was probably Hugh Boy O'Heyne).

John Cam O'Shaughnessy was slain by O'Loughlin "in a game on the green at Conrode".

1417 AD

Durlus Guaire was mentioned by Colgan in a poem addressed by Giolla Iosa Mor MacFirbis to O'Dowd of the northern Ui Fiachrach. Hugh Boy (Aodh Buidhe) or Hugh the Yellow-haired O'Heyne was followed by Brian O'Heyne and after him came Conor O'Heyne. Little was recorded of.the family after that date.

It was said that Eoghan O'Heyne built the present Dunguaire Castle at this time. However some say Edmond O'Heyne built the present castle. About this time the O'Shaughnessys' principal castles were Gortinsguaire, Ardameelavane and Fiddane which was probably built in 1520.

There is also a suggestion that Rory Mor Deary O'Shaughnessy took the castle of Doon (Guaire) from Flann Kilkelly (possibly Flann, son of Conor O'Heyne) and that he demolished it and erected another in its place called Doongorey. (Took probably means inherited as the two families were close kin).

Henry VIII was King of Ireland and his despoliation of the monasteries had occurred in both countries but the English had little success in getting the Irish to renounce the Pope. After promulgation of the Act of Supremacy the Counter Reformation actually grew in strength in Ireland. The Dissolution of the Monasteries, sometimes referred to as the Suppression of the Monasteries, was the administrative and legal process between 1536 and 1541 by which Henry VIII destroyed monasteries, priories, convents and friaries in England, Wales and Ireland and selling the land and buildings to wealthy subjects in an early form of privatisation!

Flann, son of Conor O'Heyne, had four sons from whom came four septs:

1. Edmond, ancestor of succeeding chiefs but two.

2. In 1578, Ruaidhri na Coille (Rory or Roger of the Wood), son of Flann, son of Conchobar chief of the Aidhne died. He had been distinguished for his hospitality and activity in the use of arms from the beginning of his career until he was summoned from this world. His fraternal nephew, Eoghan Mantach, son of Edmond, was elected in this place." The Four Masters.

3. Aodh (Hugh) Buidhe, the ancestor of O'Heyne of the Castle of Dunowen.

Flann O'Heyne, the ancestor of the O'Heynes of the Castle of Dunguaire.

1530 AD

Owen O'Heyne, fraternal nephew of Rory, died. During the reign of Henry VIII, Sir Roger O'Shaughnessy had surrendered his lands on a 'grant regrant' basis (hence his English knighthood). He occupied the Ui Fiachrach castle in Gort built upon the site of King Guaire's old Gort palace. The church lands at Kilmacduagh had been granted to Richard, the second Earl of Clanrickard but he never took them up.

1567 AD

Sir Roger's son, Dermot O'Shaughnessy was commended by Queen Elizabeth I for arresting the Primate of Armagh. A deed regarded as shameful by the rest of the O'Shaughnessys.

1569 AD

Sir Roger O'Shaughnessy died.

1571 AD

John O'Shaughnessy was deprived of his title by Dermot, by then regarded as a traitor by all his kinsmen.

An order of council of Connaught dated 1586, showed that Owen Murtagh O'Heyne had got into trouble for not presenting, among other lands, Caherkearney and Cratnagh. (See Lydacan Castle).
[When in after times an O Heyne was elected chief of Hy Fiachrach Aidhne, as in 1578, we find the appointment from the Lydacan branch of the family.]

The Booke of Connaught recorded Ulick Burke living in Ballylee Castle, then called Islandmore Castle. He died there in 1595.

1584 AD

Owen Murtagh O'Heyne of Dungorye was named in an indenture with other Irish chiefs. Sir John Perrot, Queen Elizabeth's representative visited Kilmacduagh monastery. Divine service ceased there. Edmond O'Heyne, son of Flann, was probably living in Dunguaire Castle at this time. In the late 16th Century O'Donnell made several raids in the territory. Kinvara and the Burren were among his targets. The unfortunate common people of the region had to suffer the depredations not only of the English conquerors but those of the neighbouring chieftains all of whom had obligations to provide for their own by regular conquests and robbery.

1585 AD

Brian Reaghe MacKilkelly, Lord of Cloghballymore lived in the Castle of Cloghballymore in Ballindereen , 3 miles from Kinvara.

1588 AD

Eoghan (Owen the Toothless) O'Heyne died. The Annals of the Four Masters recorded it thus: "A.D. 1588 Eoghan Mantach, son of Edmond, son of Flann, son of Conchobar O'Heyne, Lord of the Hy Fiachrach Aidhne, died, and his son Aodh Buidhe (Hugh the Yellow) was elected in his place."

Monsignor Fahey has written that the attitude of the O'Heyne during this time of tribulation seems to have been honourable and praiseworthy as they held English patronage in disfavour, avoiding marriage alliances with surrounding Anglo-Irish families. Despite the example of many leading Irish chieftains of the time, they disdained English honours - preferring the ancient title of "The O'Heyne" to any titles which could have been bestowed upon them by the English sovereigns. Consequently they shared the fate of their faithful clansmen, which if a sad one was not unworthy of heroic Irish Catholics.

However, Monsignor Fahey suggested that Hugh Boy O'Heyne "... showed a selfish caution considering the atrocities committed by Sir Richard Bin gham, governor of the province ... by surrendering his property on a 'grant-regrant' basis in the 30th year of Queen Elizabeth I's reign. (See Lydacan Castle).

By agreeing to 'surrender and re-grant', in capite, with the English sovereign the chiefs became property owners in their own right holding land from the King. This was a major departure from the old order in which the chieftain held the land in trust for and from his people. Socioeconomically and politically things went downhill for the peoples of Ireland from that time on.

1588 AD

That year many ships of the Spanish Armada were wrecked along the west coast of Ireland. Unfortunately some 5000 Spanish sailors may have been killed after surviving the shipwrecks along some 500 kms of Irish coastline from Antrim to Kerry.

An interesting observation was made at this time by a Spanish nobleman called Don Francisco de Cuellar, a survivor from a ship wrecked along the coast. Of the Irish he wrote 'They live in huts of straw. It is the custom of these savages to live as the brute beasts among the mountains. The men are large bodied, of handsome features and limbs, and as active as the roe deer. They do not eat oftener than once a day and this is at night; and that which they usually eat is butter with oaten bread. They drink sour milk, for they have no other drink; they do not drink water, though it is the best in the world.... in this kingdom there is neither justice nor right, and everyone does as he pleases".What a strange mixture of adulation and criticism! A fascinating account of this man's experience in Ireland after struggling ashore near Streedagh Strand in modern County Sligo can be found on the internet.

"Aodh Buidhe, son of Eoghan Mantach, son of Edmond, son of Flann O'Heyne died". This was the last entry about the family in the Annals of the Four Masters but MacFirbis gives additional material.

O'Donnell was raiding in the Burren and passed through Corcomroe, Corker Hill, and by the O'Heyne Castle of Corranrue into Kinvara with vast herds of stolen cattle. One group of his followers committed 'lamentable deeds' in Kinvara.

1608 AD

An inquisition (an enquiry) taken at Galway showed that O'Heyne territory then included Killoveragh with 45 quarters or 8640 acres, comprising most of the parish of Kinvara and considerable portions of Clarinbridge, Ardrahan and Kilmacduagh. There were 300 acres and 2 quarters in Doorus. In Kiloveragh (Coillofiachrach or Coill Ua bh fiachrach), Roo Castle, Corranrue, was spoken of. (This was a Hynes castle which fell in 1755 during the Lisbon earthquake!) The name O'Heyne was well known in Killogilleen. The castles of Dun Guaire and Lydacan were the O'Heynes principal strong¬holds at the time.

An inquisition showed O'Shaughnessy holding only 105 quarters in the barony of Kiltartan.

Conor Crone O'Heyne was living in Lydacan (or Lydican or Lydegan) Castle at this time.

Dominick D'Arcy bequeathed a life interest in some property to Farragh O'Heyne in Kiloreen. Connor Crone O'Heyne possessed Lydacan Castle and its lands but executed a deed of "Enfeoffment" to transmit portions of his lands to his son Bryan O'Heyne. He wrote:

"To all Chresten people to whom these presents shall come, Connor Crone O'Heyne of Ledigan in the county of Galway, Gent., send greeting to our Lord God Everlasting. Knowe yee, that I the said Connor, for sundry good and lawful considerations me moving, and inespecial for and in the regard and consideration both of my fatherly care and affection, as well toward my sonne Bryan O'Heyn, as toward the establishment, continuance and succession of myn inheritance and living in myn owne kindred and family, and the better insuring and supportation of the same from ingerous challenges, suits and vexations, thereunto to be at any time pretended, wherein the impotencie of age and state and declining years disabling me to imploy the mindful pains and travails thereunto behoofeful the defence and upholding of my said inheritance in nature and right belonging unto my said sonne Bryan O'Heyne, have given granted enfeoffed and confirmed like as those presents."

Here followed the grants - small indeed compared with the former territorial holdings of the family in previous centuries! The grants consisted of a third part of the cartron of Gortenshine, the fourth part of a cartron in the termon known as Ballymolfargie and Pollantlynte, and half a cartron in Corroboye. For these he asks a yearly rent from his son. "And further knowe yee, that I the said Connor Crone O'Heyne have covenanted and agreed that my said sonne Bryan shall pay unto me some rasonable rent yearly during myn owne liffe out of the before mentioned parcels, and after my decease to be to the use of him the said Bryan, his heires and assigns as aforesaidfor ever," etc. "In witness whereof I the said Connor Crone O'Heyne have hereunto put my hand and scale the 20 February 1612."
In O 'Donovan's, Notes to the Irish Annals.

O'HEYNE, A DOMINICAN HISTORIAN

During the year 1648, a John O'Heyne was born near Athenry (the Ford of the Kings), County Galway and he grew to dedicate his life as a Dominican friar. His grand-uncle was Dominic Burke, O.P., who in his time had opposed the Papal Nuncio, Giovanni Battista Rinuccini. John de Burgo, Archbishop of Tuam was his maternal grand-uncle.

Senan Crowe, O.P. of the Irish Dominicans said that Father John became historian of the Dominican Order eventually dying in Louvain in either 1713 or 1715 after writing a notable work in Latin called 'Epilogus Chronologicus' which is kept in the British Museum. Father O'Heyne was a Bachelor of Sacred Theology who studied at Burgos and Salamanca. He taught Philosophy in France and as a master of students, second and first regent, then he taught at intervals in the college of Holy Cross at Louvain where he was vicar for a year. On his first return to Ireland, by command of Father William Burke, provincial (from 1674 to 1682) he taught a large school, until he was obliged by violence of the persecution to hide and be companion for a year of the bishop of Elphin. Thereupon as he was specially sought after by the Protestants, he was thereby compelled to fly from the kingdom. On finishing his regency at Louvain, he returned home a second time, and remained there for eight years evangelising the people as prior at Urlar. Finally, exiled with the rest of the religious orders, after the various mishaps of distressful exile, he lived in Louvain at Holy Cross, in the sixtieth year of his age and the fortieth of his profession. At one time he was a candidate for bishopric of Clonfert and Kilmacduagh but was not chosen. John O'Heyne died in his sixty fifth year on 11 December 1713.

Other Irish Dominicans of the name and the era were: James Hynes, who died March 24th, 1776; John Thomas Hynes, Bishop of Leros and Apostolic Administrator of British Guiana, died March 30, 1869; Bartholomew O'Heyne, died Jan. 1, 1718. The most recent members of the order with the surname were Flannan Hynes (Provincial between 1969 and 1977) and his brother Paul Hynes.Over the years many of Guaire's descendants have entered the priesthood and religious orders and indeed today the tradition is being sustained.

During the 17th and 18th centuries, penal laws destroyed the power of the Gaelic chieftains once and for all time and along with them went the Anglo-Norman lords who adopted Irish ways. Land in the Ui Fiachrach Aidhne's territories went to the Persses, Lamberts, Martyns, Gregorys,

Taylors, etc. By this year most of the O'Heynes' property had passed into Cromwellian hands.

1645 AD

The Reverend Michael J. Hynes was one of the members of the mission of Rinuccini, nuncio extraordinary to Ireland. Another source places a Reverend Michael J. Hynes as having written a dissertation for a doctorate of Louvain University called The Mission of Rinunnici,

1647 AD

Dr. Hugh de Burgo, O.F.M., took possession of the church at Kilmacduagh and had the neglected portion of the cathedral re-roofed but by the year 1656, after de Burgo's exile, the cathedral once again fell into disuse.

Following Owen Boy O'Heyne's death in 1594, came his son, another Owen Boy and then after him his son, Eoghan of Lydacan. The Civil Survey, preserved in the Custom House, Dublin, during the 17th Century gave a list of the O'Heyne living in the barony of Kiltartan in 1641, principally in Dawros, Kinvara. They were: Edmond Owen O'Heyne, in Corbay; Conor O'Heyne, in Kinturly; Flan Boy O'Heyne, in Kinturly; Car. Turlogh O'Heyne who was mentioned in a land transaction in the Carran Parish when land held in 1641 by the proprietors: Donagh O'Brien, Conor O'Gowan, James O'Gowan, Donagh, son of Owen Mahone, son of Brien and Rossa O'Loghlen, was disposed of to Turlogh O'Hyne and Sir Redmond Everard. Farro O'Heine; Flan Boy O'Hene in Lissurduffe and Tomareagh; Teige and Edmond O'Hene in Moinkaebo and Moigh; Owen O'Hene in Funchinmore; Hugh O'Hene in Corearney; Elan mac Edmond O'Hene in Loughheurro; Farro O'Hine in Balligilligagh and Corconnogh; Turlo O'Hine in Cappamore; Edmond O'Hine in Drumon; Teige Reagh O'Haine in Ballimachkill; Car. Henry O'Hene, Donogh O'Heyne, Owen mac Teige Reagh O'Haine in Ballinaghan and Hugh boy O'Heine in Carrocurra and Crannan.

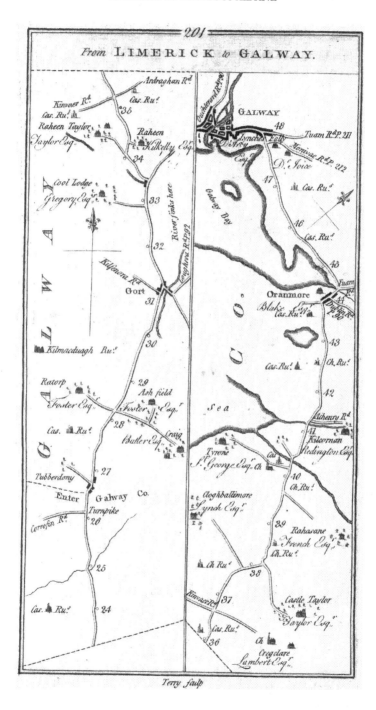

1655 AD

Sir Charles Coote banished all imprisoned priests and friars from Galway to Portugal, France, etc. and those under forty years of age as slaves to Barbados and other American plantations. The number of such Barbadosised Irish in not known but estimates vary between 60,000 and 12,000. Furthermore they were worse treated than the African slaves who had to be purchased whereas the English plantation owners go the Irish for free!

1666 AD

MacFirbis records that in the Will of Dominick Darcy (preserved in the Prerogative Court in Dublin) dated August 1, 1666, bequests were made to his brother (half brother or brother-in-law?) Farragh O'Heyne of the cartron of Kilboren with five pounds sterling to his brother Elan Boy O'Heyne, three pounds and the same sum to his brother Owen O'Heyne.

Flan Boy O'Heyne, who was living in 1641, lived in Kinturlough and his son, Peter O'Heyne was probably the last to live in the Hynes castle of Curranroe, which fell in the 1755 earthquake. Peter's son was Brian and the line continued with: John Hynes, died 1746; James Hynes, died 1802; John Hynes, born 1785 whose children were: James; Dr. Patrick Hynes of London; Thomas, died 1841 in Ardrahan; Michael, a merchant in Kinvara and John Hynes. The Kennas, descendants of this branch of the family still own Bayfield House, in New Quay, Ireland. Once a working farm it is now let as a holiday cottage. The internet site says. 'Bayfield has been owned by the Kenna family and their ancestors (the Hynes') for over 150 years and was built by the current owners' great great grandfather.'

1671 AD

Edmond O'Heyne mentioned in an O'Shaughnessy will.

1704 AD

All Popish priests were required to register after the promulgation of "An Act for Registering the Popish Clergy". All "Popish clergy" had to be registered. Among those registered in Kilmacduagh were Fathers: John Hyne, 39 years, in Carrobeg; James Hyne, 50 years, Ballylee; Denis Hyne, 37 years, Kilcolgan; Anthony Hyne, 29 years, Carirlane; Turlogh Hyne, 54 years, Poulnegan.

In that year the waters of Lough Deehan, Kilamoran, near Caherglassaun, Gort, sank very low and a wooden house was found at the bottom. Made of thick oak timber with wattle-work sides and roof it looked as if intended to float. It was thought to he one of Saint Colman's establishments.

1778 AD

At one time the O'Hynes territories stretched from Gort to Oranmore but by this time the road map by Skinner and Taylor shows the land along that road as belonging to:Gregory, Esq. (Coole Lodge); Kilkelly, Esq., a Guaire descendant, (Raheen); Taylor, Esq.; Lambert, Esq.(Croglare); French, Esq. (Rahasane); Lynch Esq.; (Cloghballymore); Redington, Esq. (Kilcoran); George, Esq. (Tyronwy); Blake, Esq. (Oranmore).

Many locusts invaded the area that year and Fr. Edward Hynes was asked by Sir Christopher St. George to rid a Protestant Church of the pests. The priest agreed to try on condition St. George became a Catholic should the prayers prove effective. They were very effective and St.George kept his word!

1798 AD

Terence Hynes was Parish Priest in Craughwell, today, a charming village with statues of Lady Gregory and the blind poet Raftery.

Kinvara: The Seaport

The ballad writer Francis Fahy set the 'Ould Plaid Shawl'... "not far from Kinvara in the merry month of May". Kinvarra [Irish: Cinn Mhara, meaning "head of the sea"], is a tidal port on a Bay bearing the name, an inlet in the south-eastern corner of Galway Bay. It lies in the barony of Kiltartan in the County of Galway.

Joyce, in his topographical work ' Irish Names of Places' wrote: "The highest point reached by the tide in a river was sometimes designated by the term ceann-mara', i.e. the head of the sea; from a spot of this kind on the River Roughty, the town of Kenmare, in Kerry, received its name; and Kinvarra in Galway, originating in the same way, for the Four Masters call it 'Ceannhara'.

Exports of grain and imports of seaweed for use as a fertilizer were carried from there in boats called hookers which still sail in and out of the port from a quay about 50 yards long, built in 1773 by J. Ffrench, Esq., great-grandfather of Baron de Basterot. The baron then lived in nearby Doorus House where he was associated with the Gaelic Revival and its exponents: W.B. Yeats and Lady Gregory. The quay was constructed from the stones of yet another O'Heynes Castle which had stood on the south side of the inlet opposite the Castle of Dunguaire probably where Delamaine Lodge now stands. It seems a pity that such a picturesque monument of the past should have been dismantled and put to such use, albeit a very practical one. A large portion of the estates at Kinvara were bought by Robert Gregory in 1769 from that James Ffrench. In the town are some remains of an old church, which was once the burial-place of the O'Heynes and Magraths; no others being allowed to be interred within its walls.
In the past, the leading representatives of the O'Hynes, Kilkellys and O'Shaughnessys were accorded the privilege of interment within the sacred precincts of the church of Cil Ua Fiachrach at Kinvara.

Today, visitors and citizens alike love to take part in the Cruinniú na mBád ("Gathering of the Boats") held in mid August when hooker races are held over several days to raise money for charity The event recalls the time when the hookers, special sailing boats, were used for trading between Kinvara, western County Galway and the north of County Clare. Turf was also imported in these hookers into Kinvara from the west of County Galway while barley, lime and timber were exported from Kinvara. The town also holds an Irish music festival, Fleadh na gCuach ("The Cuckoo Festival") on the First of May, the old Gaelic celebration of Beltaine.

THE CASTLES

Hardly castles but it is appropriate here to mention a typical Burren ringfort constructed of dry stone walling and roughly circular in shape bearing the name Cahir Baile Ui hEidhne [The seat of the people of O Heyne] It was probably a medieval farm settlement, one of about 450 such to be found in the Burren It lies in a field near the shore close to the road to the fishing village of Ballyvaughan.

DUNGUAIRE CASTLE

Near the port are extensive caverns and potholes and farther away is the interesting Aillwee Cavern at Ballyvaughan. Half a mile to the north east of the port, close to the junction of the road to Kilcolgan and the road to Ardrahan stands Dun Guaire Castle, a sixteenth century fortified towerlet surrounded by a bawn, a defensive wall. It now enjoys the distinction of being the most photographed castle in Ireland. Dun Guaire is quite a landmark which can be seen for miles out to sea. It rises from a rocky promontory, a dun, the foundations of which are licked by the waters of the Bay, in which swim dignified swans. Joyce wrote: "Half a mile east of Kin varra, on the seashore stands an ancient circular fort all that remains of the hospitable palace of Durlas. The present castle, a tower house, built by the O'Heyne stands near the very site of the house of Guaire the Hospitable". The 'modern' castle has not been built within the old fort, the remains of which are hidden under centuries of earth on a slight rise about fifty yards to the north. Whether or not the present castle stands on exactly the same spot is open to doubt but it certainly stands very close to the ancient palace, and, within a stone's throw, on a smaller neck of land, slightly to the south stand the remains of a building of indefinite age with an interesting stone arch of superior craftsmanship which is probably early medieval. The archway still standing, is surrounded by fallen masonry of a solid character predating the Hynes castle. It stands on cavernous rock-strewn ground fordable at low tide. The archway could be all that remains of the 13th century Kinvara Castle which was demolished and its stones used in the construction of the present Dunguaire Castle. All that is left of the old Kinvara Castle is the well defined stone archway on the small spit of land near the present castle. On an opposite shoreline on the bay, there may have been an early castle called Ballybranaghan Castle standing until the year, 1615, in what are now the grounds of the house called Delamaine Lodge.

In the 18th.century, some of the schooners riding at anchor in the bay would have carried contraband which may well have been landed at Delamaine Lodge built on the site of the old castle and home of the smuggler, the Huguenot protestant, Captain De Lemaine. An early instance of the brotherhood of smugglers made up of Protestant and Catholic enthusiasts defying the state. Thus, Kinvara made a name for itself in the 1700's by defying the Excise men in the illicit importation of fine wines, tobacco and brandy. Mysterious cargoes were stored in the district during the excise seizures of 1792.

Recent owners of Delamaine Lodge, have found evidence of a cobbled area in the grounds; a courtyard, once surrounded by a bawn, parts of which form some of the garden walls in Delamaine. He has also discovered fine, well cut slabs which are very like the lintels in the windows of Dunguaire. Even the same punched dot decorative motif appears on the slabs. One day, perhaps, the secret tunnel, which according to local tradition, leads from the shore into the house will be rediscovered! The cavernous nature of the ground certainly makes the presence of such a tunnel possible; it may even be the run of an old underground river.

Old maps use the name Ballybranaghan for the ground upon which Delamaine is built. In 1641, Ballybranaghan belonged to Edmund O'Heyne but it became the property of Colonel Dillon after the land seizures designed to dispossess the old 'popish' chieftains. James Frost, Clare historian, mentioned having known a descendant of the O'Heyne who had lived in the Castle of Ballybranaghan.

THE KING'S BANQUET

The good King Guaire's legendary hospitality was regularly exercised in supplying the frequent guests with a sumptuous array of food during banquets. According to George Brandon Saul in Traditional Irish Literature and its Backgrounds, the foods available were: venison and other meats roasted on peeled hazelwood spits; meats boiled in bronze cauldrons or baked in pits of hot stones; roasted or griddled meat, basted with honey; honey too, taken with milk. Among the meats would have been beef, pork, mutton, badger and hare. Then perhaps, choice salmon, birds and their eggs, cabbage, leeks, onions, watercress nettles, garlic, seaweed (from the coastal rocks). All eaten in season.

The available fare was more extensive still, with: fruits, apples, nuts, griddle cakes, porridge, wheat, barley, oatmeal, buttermilk (mixed with honey for the King's son), fresh butter for the King and salted butter for the others. The ale was brewed from barley malt and was carried in waggons on raids. Mead was also drunk and in later years wine too.

The 'Crith Gabbach' had this to say of the royal banqueting hall. The King should sit on the north side while his mercenaries sit on the south side. These mercenaries must not be men spared from death in battles in case they still harboured grievances against the King and should so prove dangerous. Such men should be those whom the King had saved from violent death or from capture by their enemies as such men are most likely to remain loyal. There should be at least four of these bodyguards: a front guardsman, a rear guardsman, and one for each flank. The bodyguards should accompany the King as he enters and as he leaves the banqueting hall.

The 'base' clients who join the King at the feast should be the kind of men who each owns land worth seven cumala 'bondswomen', the name given to a coin with a value of 3 milch cows. Such men must be responsible people with duties related to the King's chattels, to the church and to law.

To the west of the King, in the hall, sit the envoys and behind them sit their guest companies and the poets with harpers behind them in turn. On the south-east side sit pipers, horn players and jugglers. Then on the north side should stand a warrior, the King's champion guarding the door with his spear in hand ready to stop disturbances in the banqueting hall.

The nobles would sit on the west side in close attendance to the King. Hostages should be seated behind them and the judge would take up his position there. To the west of the king should sit the Queen. On the north west side, in chains, would sit the forfeited hostages!

BANQUETS AT DUNGUAIRE TODAY

Today, throughout the summer months within the present Dunguaire Castle, the past is re-lived, again and again, when paying guests from all over the world assemble for the nightly banquets set out by the Shannon Free Airport Development Company whose property the castle now is. After the feast, the Shannon Castle Entertainers provide a programme of literary entertainment of extracts from famous Irish writers such W.B. Yeats, John M. Synge and Sean O'Casey. Naturally, Irish music and song are also included in the evening's entertainment.

Dunguaire is also open to day visitors during the holiday months between mid April and mid October.

DUNGUAIRE CASTLE

Of the present castle, O'Donovan's Survey had this to say: 'This castle was erected on the site of the palace of Guaire Aidhne, King of Connaught, the ancestor of the O'Heynes who erected several other castles in the vicinity'. An article in Volume 49 of the Royal Society of Antiquaries states that Martyn (The Martins occupied the castle after the expulsion of the Hynes in the mid-seventeenth century) cleared the ground around the present castle to look for evidence of earlier occupation finding nothing but mortar built walls. There was, however, across a shallow creek, an early remarkable fort in the townland of Dungoora east beside an outflow from an underground river and that may have been the Durlas of King Guaire of Connaught. The outflow, fresh water, can be seen bubbling up and into the seawater. A scooped handful tastes fresh after having travelled for miles under the cavernous ground from Coole Lake, a turlough which never empties entirely during summer but falls in depth as it empties into the underground caverns below the park commemorated in Yeats's poem Coole Park 1929.

These underground flooded passages are sometimes as much as 25 metres in diameter carrying fresh water to large springs near Dun Guaire castle. Inland , collapsed hollows such as the Devil's Punch Bowl, a bottomless agitated pool, near Gort may be found giving access to intrepid cavers along lengths of the underground river and the Beagh River which flows from the lake at Coole Park and from Lough Cutra.

Opinions vary as to which of the O'Heynes actually built this Norman tower house, one of the many hundreds of such places erected during the reign of Henry the Eighth of England who was giving grants of fifty pounds in some areas of Ireland to those who undertook the building of such fortified residences. Three or four different chieftains have been suggested as builders of Dunguaire Castle: Owen Muirchetach O'Heyne, Edmund O'Heyne, Flann O'Heyne and Rory O'Shaughnessy. The mystery of the three different builders may be solved if it is supposed that each of the three chieftains had their own castles on Kinvara Bay: Dunguaire Castle, Ballybranaghan Castle and Kinvara Castle.

It was probably built in the year 1520 A.D. Others have suggested that during the reign of Hen. VIII, Rory More Darag O'Shaughnessy took the castle of Doon from Flan Killikelly, totally demolished it, and erected one near its site, which he named Doongorey.

The dun, in Kinvara, has been a fortification for some 13 centuries and during that time much fresh water has flowed through the underground rivers into the Bay of Galway and much water has flowed under political bridges. So too many an armed struggle has taken place within a day's march of the present castle. As previously mentioned, the battles between rival O'Connor princes centred around the monastery of Kilmacduagh during the 13th Century and the proximity of Dunguaire to the pass at Corker Hill (Corcair na Cleraech) meant the involvement of the O'Heyne chieftains in the struggles between Connaught and Thomond.

Some three centuries later, in 1594, during the Nine Years war, O'Donnell set out from Ballymote, in today's County Sligo, and by moving rapidly arrived secretly in Clanrickard territory. The inhabitants of the country were not entirely surprised by this attack as they lived in a constant state of fear of such attacks by him. After arriving at the gate of Kilcolgan, O'Donnell launched his forces upon the population. His bands of marauding mercenaries plundered in every direction. One group set out for the Slieve Aughty hills and others attacked Kinvarra. At Isert Kelly, the attackers made William MacHubert prisoner, while at Dunguaire they killed Turlough Boy O'Loughlin and his brother Bryan, both sons of Ross O'Loughlin. Two sons of William Burke of Renville were also slain together with a son of Theobald Burke of Derry Donnell.

In 1595, O'Donnell again raided the territory attacking Dunguaire in the vicinity of which 'lamentable deeds" were done according to the Annals. O'Donnell returned to Sligo with many spoils of war and large herds of stolen cattle. That year and back in Sligo, Red Hugh O'Donnell demolished the castle there to prevent it falling into the hands of the English whom he hated and resisted; with good reason as they were land grabbing invaders.

One would have thought that there would have been little left to plunder after that but he again mounted attacks on the district. In fact he plundered the district for three successive years: 1594, 1595 and 1596. After camping near the castle of Dunkellin, two miles from Kilcolgan during the summer of one year, he attacked Kinvarra again, devastating the whole of the Burren. Later he raided, plundering ' ... the counties that lay on both sides of Sliab Echtge (Slieve Aughty), and especially Thomond. The Annalists wrote: "All the country behind them as far as they could see on either side, was enveloped in one dark cloud of vapour and smoke, and during the entire of the day the vastness of the dark clouds of smoke that rose over them aloft in every place to which they directed their course was enough to set them astray on their route'.

Although the O Heyne had hitherto resisted all offers of knighthoods from the Tudor monarchs, Hugh Boy O'Heyne now surrendered his lands on 'grant regrant' to the British Crown in in 1594. In doing so he also contributed to the end of the old Gaelic order in which the land belonged to all the clan and not solely and privately to the chieftain. He must have been living in either Dunguaire and Lydacan at the time. Some years earlier, his father, Owen Murtagh O'Heyne, living in Dunguaire in 1585, and also in Lydacan, failed to declare certain lands to the Crown but the position had been 'regularised' by an Order of Council of Connaught in 1586."Whereas, it is given to understand that Owen Mantagh O'Hein of Lydegane, in the barony of Kilaraght, within the County)' of Galway, chiefe of his name, is seized among other lands of the quarter of land called Caherkearney, and the quarter of Cratnagh which 2 quarters by a reason were not presented to us are not comprised within the Indentures of Her Majesties Composition, andforas much as by the said Indentures there was no freedom provided for the said Owen, and that by his own confession and presentment it is found that the said two quarters be concealed and not presented as afforesaid, whereby he is the better worthie to engage the same. It is therefore condescended, granted and agreed in consideration of the premises that the said Owen Mantagh O'Hein shall possess said lands discharged of her Majesties Composition Rent. Given at Dublin the 13th

May, 1586.Richard Bingham, Thomas Dillon, Thomas C. Strange, George Comerford, Nicholas White

Hugh-the-Yellow O'Heyne succeeded Owen the Toothless O'Heyne after the death of the latter in 1588, the year of the Armada. According to Kelly, writing in the Royal Society of Antiquarians Journal, the reference in O'Flaherty's West Connaught is to Oene Mantagh O'Heine of Dungorye.

The State of Ireland in 1598 mentions Martyn as owner Tullira Castle, formerly a Burke stronghold. About fifty years later they were living in Dunguaire Castle.

The castle site does show up on John Speed's map of Munster dated 1610 under the name 'O'Henes' although after 1615 there seemed to be no O'Hynes living in Dunguaire despite the fact that another map by W. Hole, dated 1637, was still showing 'O'Henes' at the head of the bay. Cartographers must have kept the traditional name for quite some time after the expulsion of the O'Heyne.

In 1603 much of Ireland was still held by descendants of the Anglo-Norman invaders but very little was still in the hands of the old Gaelic families. By the end of the century almost all land had been taken by Protestant British adventurers and the native Irish reduced to landless servants. This was the period of the Plantations in Ulster and the end of the era of the Irish Chieftains. Before very long the O'Heynes were ousted from their castles, some seven of them, in their traditional territory. It has been speculated that the O'Heynes must have ceded Dunguaire to the Clanrickarde Burkes very early in the 17th Century, for, one Oliver Martin was holding the castle of them in 1607. The Martins had been early settlers in the 'Citie of the Tribes', Galway itself and were Catholics so the question of seizure hardly arises or does it?

Kelly quotes from a letter, received from the Right Hon. Archer Martin, a judge of the Appeal Court of British Columbia, who died in 1941, in an article, which appeared in an issue of the Royal Society of Antiquaries of Ireland:'In the Record Office, among the grants pursuant to Privy Seal, there is one dated at Westminster, February 21st, 1615, to Oliver Martin, of Kinvarra, gentleman of the Castle of Kinvarra and parcels of Kinvarra,

Ballybranegan and Knocknechollin, containing 1 quarter in the Barony of Kiltaraght in the county of Galway, to hold of the Earl of Clanrickard, by the like tenure as by inquisition taken at Loghreogh, 6th September,1607'.

Kelly also suggested that Richard Martin must have bought the castle from the O'Heynes as no forfeiture was hinted at nor any marriage between the two families. According to the novelist Charles F. Blake-Forster in The Irish Chieftains and Their Struggle For the Crown, Richard Martin got Dunguara Castle near Kinvarra from the chief of the sept of O'Hynes and that Martin's first residence in the area was in that castle and that he was later granted Tullira by King Charles. The whole matter is somewhat confused over when and under what circumstances the castle passed out of the hands of the O'Hynes.

Catholics lost the power to vote and were prevented from owning large estates.The Land Purchase Act had as its objective the prevention of the further growth of 'Popery'. Perhaps the Martins did 'buy' Dunguaire from the O'Heyne. The new rulers of Ireland said; " Oliver Martin of Tulliry, Co. Galway, Esquire, was, during the rebellion, a person who behaved himself with great moderation, and was remarkably kind to numbers of Protestants in distress, many of whom he supported in his family, and by his charity and goodness saved their lives, and so on, enacted that he might enjoy his estates to him and his heirs, and settle and dispose of the same to his eldest son and heirs male."

In 1642, Richard Martin, Mayor of Galway, was living in Dunguaire. He was a counsellor at law and the ancestor of the Tullira Martins. The castle stayed in the hands of the Martins for some considerable time afterwards, although the Martins, with others, lost much of their land as a result of the Land Purchases Act of 1691 during the Williamite Settlement. New penal laws against Catholics were passed so that by 1700 only some 300,000 acres, about 5% of Ireland was in the hands of Catholics. From then on Catholics were excluded from towns and from the professions. They were disarmed and clergy were forced to leave; some had been placed in concentration camps on islands off the Irish coast, while others were shipped off like common felons and slaves to the British colonies. For example in the early 18th, century the number of 'Barbadosised' Irish slaves could have been as high as 60,000 or as low as 12,000, if one can think of 12,000 as low!

Whilst it is written that Richard Martin "...got Dunguara Castle from the chief of the sept of O Heynes" in 1642 , it is possible that some thirty years earlier than Richard,   Oliver Martin may have occupied another Hynes castle which may have been called Ballybranaghan Castle, situated on ground now occupied by Delamaine Lodge. One must suppose that as relations between the Martins and O'Heynes were good and purchase was made in each case. In a document dated 1703 Oliver Martin was cited as a godparent of Dominic O' Heyne who was applying for a commission the Spanish army. See below under Cahererillan Castle.

The Cromwellians banished the Catholic Hynes but allowed the Catholic Martins to stay in the area because they had protected Protestants `in distress. Nevertheless much of the Martin land was given to a Colonel Carey Dillon who also held land in the Barony of Ibrickan, County Clare. At the same time we find that Edmund O'Hene and Shane McEdmond O'Hene having to give up land; some of which went to the same Colonel Dillon and some to Walter Taylor.

In Lady Gregory's book on Kiltartanese there is a reference "The English were feasting at Cillin O' Guaire till the time Sarsfield came." That could have been at a time after King James had appointed the Irish born Sarsfield to help re-organise the Irish army or later in about 1689 after helping secure Connaught for the Jacobites.

Dunguaire was badly shaken at the time of the earthquake of 1755 and one wonders who was living there at the time as they must have had quite a fright as another of their clan castles in Corrarue, a few miles along the coast, fell into a heap of rubble. Elsewhere, in an article on Dunguaire by R.J. Kelly (R.S.A. 1913) it is said that the castle became the property of Thomas Taylor who encircled it with a bawn. It is more likely that Taylor rented the place from Martyn who according to Kelly took pride in keeping the place in a good state of preservation especially when there was no one living there and a caretaker was employed to take care of the fabric of the old building.

As the Martins had chosen to live in Tullira, they let the castle of Dunguaire to tenants, among whom were Colonel Daly of Raford and his family in 1787 but by 1828 a British garrison, not a family, was living there.

Certainly in the 19th century various Hynes families were still living in the district. For example Denis Hynes was the lessor of several business premises in the town of Kinvara at the time of Griffith's Valuation. O'Connell states that Denis Hynes eventually purchased Seamount House from the Butlers in the late 1840s and that it was his daughter who gave it to the Mercy Nuns in 1921. According to genealogical information he was Dr. Denis Joseph Hynes and members of his wife's family are buried in the cemetery adjoining the abbey at Corcomroe, County Clare. Further away, in the 1870s John Hynes and William J. Hynes both of Ballinasloe owned over 4,000 acres in County Roscommon, mainly in the parish of Creagh, barony of Moycarn. They appear to have bought the estate from the Kellys of Creagh. An estate of over 2,700 acres belonging to the John W. Hynes in county Roscommon was sold to the Congested Districts' Board in June 1913.

By 1924, the castle had begun to fall into ruins so that by the time it was bought by Oliver St. John Gogarty, surgeon, poet and author, as a romantic place of retreat it was in desperate need of restoration. Gogarty intended to repair the place ready for occupation but he never actually got around to living there himself so he eventually sold the castle to Christabel Lady Ampthill who restored Dunguaire and lived there for many years.

In the late 1920s Christabel Lady Ampthill hit the national headlines when she was involved in lengthy and costly proceedings in the English courts of law against her husband, Lord Russell who sought divorce claiming that Christabel's child was not his own because the marriage was never consummated! Eventually the courts ruled that her baby, born in 1921, was indeed that of her husband. Although Christabel agreed that the marriage was never fully consummated holding that the nearest Russell ever achieved, said she were 'Hunnish scenes', incomplete intercourse. During the trial the populace were making jokes about her being a kind of aristocratic Virgin Mary! Speculation continued for years afterwards but, in her book, Christabel: Russell Case and After, Eileen Hunter wrote that she believed Christabel had lived and died without having a complete sexual relationship with any man.

Christabel bought Dunguaire castle. Eileen Hunter recounted that when Christabel first saw Dunguaire, the enormous original fireplace was still intact and she became enchanted with both it and the entire building. So, with the help of an architect, Christabel set about the costly and time-consuming task of restoration, during which she managed to combine the ancient charm of the place with an array of modern comforts. She added central heating making the castle better than comfortable. In fact, wrote Eileen Hunter, one unnamed guest found his room so intolerably hot that he threw a riding boot at the turret window to break it and allow some air into the room.

It was during 1964, when Christabel was supervising the re-roofing of Dunguaire, that a stranger came upon the scene. This mysterious stranger showed an uncanny interest in the work and an uncanny knowledge of both the building methods used and of the architecture. What is more the stranger begged to be allowed to pay the entire cost of the new roofing. Hunter wrote, "Who he was, neither I nor anyone else has been told, but were it not unusual for a phantom to proffer a gift of money that did not vanish at daybreak like the 'fairy gold' in many an Irish legend and had the experience not happened to Christabel.... I have dismissed the tale as an excursion into Gaelic phantasy." Perhaps King Guaire's right arm had grown a little longer after that occasion!

Christabel was a great horsewoman in her time and she kept a stable at Dunguaire where she trained the horses. No doubt the spirits of the O'Heynes " of the beautiful slender steeds" would have been with her looking on with approval.

A DESCRIPTION OF DUNGUAIRE CASTLE TODAY

Most Irish tower houses in Galway and Clare were made of limestone with rough unwrought or hammer dressed rubble within the walls and chiselled stones at the quoins and corners of doors and windows. The bawn of this castle was actually rebuilt in 1642 having existed before that date. Within this encompassing wall stands the tower house itself, one of the many built in the west of Ireland in which the Gaelic aristocracy once lived. The tower is a three-storey building with its principal rooms above. The two lower storeys have their original fireplaces and one of these was made into a drawing room for Lady Ampthill while the other became a dining room. One principal addition only was the unobtrusive two-storey wing joining the main tower to the towerlet or the lookout post.

THE BAWN

The courtyard is surrounded by a high wall called a bawn. The bawn has very little defensive strength but it served to contain livestock and men at arms in small barracks. Sentries could patrol the walls along stone walkways which were often extended inwards by planks supported by struts. Centuries ago the courtyard would have held stables, servants quarters and livestock. During the early twentieth century, Lady Christabel Ampthill kept horses within the bawn as did the chieftains centuries before.

CASTLE WALLS

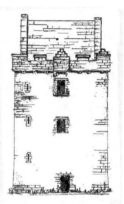

The eastern wall of Dunguaire Castle faces the courtyard. It is about 35 feet [10.6m] long and 50 feet high [15.1m], from ground to battlements. At its highest point, the top of the gable facing the shore, is 65 feet [19.7m]. Standing as the castle does on elevated ground, its height above sea level is considerably more. The stonework jutting out above the windows is called machicolation. An aperture in it made it possible for defenders on the roofwalks to drop missiles on the heads of attackers.

BATTLEMENTS AND PARAPETS

The view from the top of the tower includes Kinvara Bay to the west, from which in the evenings you can see the sun go down on Galway Bay! To the southwest, the Burren hills rise before you in limestone splendour. Eastwards lies the great plain of the Ui Fiachrach Aidhne, home of the descendants of King Guaire, the Hospitable. Many castle parapets were crenellated in the Irish style and these at Dunguaire may have been crenellated in that manner but during restoration the present pattern replaced them. The openings in the bottom of the parapet immediately above the windows would have made it possible for defenders to drop injurious objects upon attackers trying to get in through doors below.

WINDOWS

Chiselled stones were used at the corners of castle walls and at the edges of doors and windows. The stones around Dunguaire's windows are decorated with punched dots similar to those on the window slabs found in the grounds of Delamaine Lodge. The windows are square headed and chamfered. Other castles in the area have more elegant stonework patterns. Small apertures allowed light into various levels of the staircase within. On looking out of the window towards the shore, you may see the fresh water bubbling up from the caverns below to mingle with the sea.

CHIMNEYS

Chimneys rose from the gables or from sidewalls. There were fireplaces in the corners of the west walls of Dunguaire on the second floor and a fireplace in the northwest corner of the first floor. There may have been a chimney in the southwest corner at one time.

ROOF AND ATTIC

The roofs of Irish tower houses were high pitched, made of timber and covered with stone slabs, slates or wooden shingles. Thatch would have been uncommon as it could easily have been fired by attackers from without or by kitchen fires from within for the attic would have contained the kitchen and cooking area.

ALURE

The alure is the narrow walkway around the roof and attic within the defensive parapet. Rainwater from the roof would have dripped onto the outwardly inclined alure slabs to run away through gaps in the parapet.

THE TOWERLET

At the southwestern corner of the courtyard there stands a guard room or towerlet now joined to the keep or main tower by an extension built this century. There may have been other towerlets in previous centuries

THE GROUND FLOOR

The vaulted ground floor or cellar is 18 feet 10 ins. [5.7m] long by 15 feet 3 ins.[4.6m] wide. At ground level the walls are 9'6" [2.8m] thick at the southern end and about 7' 6"[2.2m] thick elsewhere. The small door in the eastern wall would not have been there in Tudor times. Windows at this level would have been foolish weaknesses in the defences. A porter or doorkeeper would have had charge of this ground floor room where the provisions would have been kept.

VAULTING

It was customary for Irish tower houses to have at least one vaulted chamber, often the lowest room or cellar but sometimes an upper room aswell. Wickerwork mats and timbers were used in the construction of these £50 Tudor castles. Woven wickerwork basketry mats were used as supports for the vaulting during building work, while the mortar was wet. This pliable matting could be used very effectively to form the shape of the archway by acting as a base upon which was laid the mortar and the voussoirs, stones of the vaulting. When the mortar was dry, the wickerwork and the timber supports were removed to leave a freestanding archway. On its removal, pieces of willow rod were often left embedded in the mortar and some of those rods can be seen to this very day as may the marks left by the mats.

SPIRAL STAIRCASE

The first floor up is reached by climbing a spiral staircase lit by arrow slits or loopholes. Defenders coming down the stairs had a sword arm advantage as the treads are wider on their right; whereas right handed attackers ascending were disadvantaged trying to wield their weapons where the tread was narrowest. In some tower houses the stairs gave sword advantage to left handed defenders. The MacNamaras near Limerick may have been left-handed!

THE FIRST FLOOR

The external walls at first floor level have been reduced to a maximum thickness of 5' 6" [1.6m] at the northernmost end and only 1' 6" [0.4m] at the southern end. There would have been a murder hole in the floor of this room to drop lethal objects or weapons onto attackers getting through the door on the ground floor. The room is at least 17' [5.1m] long and 12' [3.6m] wide excluding the alcoves. There is one fireplace in the northwest corner.

SECOND FLOOR

On the second floor the walls are about 4 feet [1.2m] thick uniformly. There are two fireplaces; one at the north-west corner and another in the south-west corner. This room is about 17 [5.1m] feet long by 13 feet [3.9m] wide. Floors of upper rooms were supported by heavy oaken beams, 12 to 14 inches [0.3m] across. They, in turn, rested on wall plate timbers which ran close to the walls and themselves resting on stone corbels projecting from the huge walls inside.

A wall an the south side of Dunguaire, now partly hidden by the 'new' two storey wing once had a 13 foot [4m] high external archway 'which at some time has been filled with dressed stones. There must ,at one time ,have been a large vaulted room on that south side of the castle, probably when the castle was newly built. The present rooms between that wall and the towerlet are part of a modern addition.

THE OLD ARCH ON THE SHORE

A well defined arch, the sole remains of a large 13th.century castle built by the O'Heyne after the loss of their castle at Ardrahan, stands on the neck of land close to Dunguaire Castle. It must, at one time, have been strong enough to defy demolition carried out during the 16th. century when the 13th. century castle was razed to the ground to provide building material for Dunguaire. The archway is typical 13th.century Anglo Norman and it was probably centred with beams and planks in the Irish manner. It has been said that Rory O'Shaughnessy demolished a castle at Kinvara in the early 16th. century and this may have been it.

Dunguaire , now the most photographed castle in Ireland, was used as a filming location for the Scottish castle home of the main character in the 1979 film *North Sea Hijack* starring Roger Moore, James Mason and Anthony Perkins. It was portrayed as the Scottish home of an eccentric naval officer training a commando unit.

Lewis's Topographical Dictionary of Ireland says of Kinvara, 'A castle stood near the pier but its materials have been used in building'. That castle was another O'Hyne fort which once stood on the edge of the Bay, opposite Dunguaire , but its stones were used in the extension of the pier in the late 18th. century. Monsignor Fahey, priest, and historian, wrote : "...one of the fine old castles which flung their shadows on the little harbour was thrown down to supply building materials for the erection of the existing pier alongside of which schooners of fair tonnage my safely ride at anchor."

According to local tradition, a secret tunnel runs below ground from the Delamaine Lodge to the shore. It was said to have been used by the smuggler Captain DeLaMaine, a Huguenot, who lived at the lodge running a joint Huguenot Protestant / Irish Catholic enterprise in defiance of British law!

It would be difficult to delineate the boundaries of the Ui Fiachrach of Guaire's time but it certainly was extensive and it certainly reached into Munster. In an ancient story, Tain Bo Regomon, the ford of Ath cliath Meadhraighe, near Clarinbridge is placed within Aidhne lands. Clarinbridge was thought to be the western end of the mythologically significant Great Road, Eiscir Riada, from Dublin to the west. White Horse Hill was the actual end where an ancient solar god galloped off. MacFirbis says that the traditional northern boundary was on the edge of O'Flaherty country hard up against the city of Galway. Eastwards the Ui Fiachrach went as far as Moenmoy, southwestwards to Cineal Fearmaic in Thomond and westwards to the Burren and the shores of the Bay of Galway. Coil Ua bh fiachrach, the wood of the Ui Fiachrach, Kiloveragh, was a central O'Hynes area. After the regularisation of the diocesan boundaries, the diocese of Kilmacduagh corresponded exactly with the Ui Fiachrach territories. To help defending what was left of these territories during the sixteenth and early seventeenth centuries the O'Heynes, the O'Shaughnessys and the Kilkellys built castles, tower houses there within easy reach of each other.

The O Heyne had at least three fortifications on Kinvara Bay along with another at Curranroe just 4 miles away, now a mere pile of rubble on the seashore, on the coast road, the N67. Then, a few miles inland there was Lydacan on an approach road from Kinvarra towards the N18 trunk road where Ardrahan castle once stood. Just two miles or so south of Kinvara rose up Cahererillan Castle and Caherglissane or Caherglassaun, 2 miles SSE of Kinvara. It is likely that Killinny (Possibly 'Kil hEidhne') Castle could have been another as was Dunowen. All of these were within easy reach of their kinsmen's castles, those of the O'Shaughnessys and Kilkennys.

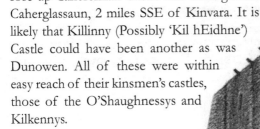

LYDACAN

Lydacan Castle, an O'Heyne tower house, could have been erected in the 14th century but was probably built during Tudor times. It is likely that during the reign of Henry VIII, Lydacan (Lydican or Lydegane) was the

O'Hynes most easterly fortification while Burkes strongholds lay further to the east and the O'Shaughnessys lay closer to Gort. Both Dunguaire and Lydacan were in the hands of Owen Murtagh O'Heyne during the latter part of the 16th Century as Owen succeeded Rory of the Wood in 1578. Hugh Boy O'Heyne followed his father , Owen, as Lord of the Ui Fiachrach Aidhne surrendering his lands and castles to the Crown in the thirtieth year of the reign of Queen Elizabeth I. In return, the O'Heynes received a royal grant of the same territory on the usual conditions of service of a military nature as given here:

"A graunte unto Hughe Boy O'Heine, sonne and heire of One (Owen) O'Heyne of Ledigan, in the County of Galway, within the province of Connaught, upon his surrender, bearing date the 22nd of July in the XXXth yeare of her Majesties raigne, of 33s. 4d. Sterlinge yerely, chief rent going out of three quarters of lande in Crannaghe, of one quarter of lande in Clonchie of one quarter of lande in Caherne, one quarter of lande in Cahircarne, one quarter of land in Crossye, and two quarters of lande in Rahassane; and also 22s. 4d. Ster. chiefe rent yerely going out of one quarter of lande in Sisselleidigan, one quarter of lande in Tuelgon, one quarter of lande in Dun guoire, in the aforesaid Countie: also 33s. 4d. chiefe rent yerely goinge out of one quarter lande of Caherkillen, one quarter of lande in Cahermadorishe, one quarter of lande in Powleneveigh and one quarter of land in Rahalben in the aforesaid Countie; also 33s. 4d. Ster. chiefe rent yerely goinge out of one quarter of lande in Ballibuige, one quarter of lande in Lawghcoure, one quarter of lande in Kiltawne, and one quarter of lande in Caherscarlie in the aforesaid countie; also fortie one shillings foure pence Ster. chiefe rent yerely going out of one quarter of lande in Ballevanegrane one quarter of lande in Monsecrib, one quarter of lande in le Mey, one quarter of lande in Fonchenbeg, one quarter of lande in Keapaghmore and one quarter of lande in Clogher in the aforesaid countie. also 35s. 8d. Ster. chiefe rent yerely going out of one quarter of lande in Knocklegan, one quarter of lande in Gortevallaile, one quarter of lande in Dromyn, one quarter of lande in Trelick one quarter of lande in fonshemore, one quarter of lande in Rewe, one quarter of lande in Dowres, one quarter of lande in Agart, one quarter of lande in Balliglara, one quarter of lande in Killily, and one quarter of lande in Cloneste in the aforesaid countie. Summa total X pounds Ster. to the said Hughe O'Heine and his heires and assignes for ever per servicum Militare, viz, per servicium XXme. partis unius feodi Militis. Solvo jure cujuslibet. Delierat. in Cane. Hibernie xxiii Julii. an.r.Eliz.xxx, tempore Wil. Fitzwilliams."

(It is possible that at the time a quarter of land was about 120 acres or four cartrons of 30 acres each.)

This Hugh Boy died in 1594 and he is the last mentioned in theAnnals of the Four Masters. During the lordship of Owen Murtagh O'Heyne, a Nehemias Fallane was searching land ownership in Connaught and it was discovered that some chiefs, among them Owen, had submitted inaccurate records. The order of Council of 1586 enabled "the Lord of Lydegane and Dungory' to keep his lands including Cranna and Cahireanna which lie close to the castle of Lydacan.

Connor Crone O'Hynes lived in Lydacan Castle in the year 1612 and he was thought to be the brother of the previous lord. This Connor lived to be over one hundred years of age and before his death he executed a deed of enfeoffment to pass as much of his land as he could securely do onto his son Bryan O'Hynes. However shortly afterwards the estate was divided up and passed onto other members of the family, among them Donnell O'Hynes who was a freeholder in the ancient territory of Kiloveragh in the year 1615. By 1641, there were at least 13 families with the name O'Hynes in Kinvarra and in Doorus and that year marked not only the end of an Ireland which their forebears had known but also the end of their power as Lords of Ui Fiachrach Aidhne.

There is an interesting note in Fairbairns Crests (1968) where it is given that the Killikellys from Bilbao, Spain, had been granted a coat of arms in 1772 having claimed descent from Murtagh Killikelly (O'Heyne) of the Castle of Lydacan in County Galway. The arms were granted to Brian or Bernard Killikclly said to have been fourth in descent from Murtagh. There may be some confusion of this when the details are compared with the entries under Cahererillan Castle.

LYDACAN CASTLE

The ruined castle of Lydacan lies four and a half miles from Dunguaire off the road leading east south-east through Loughcurra at about a mile along the road past the crossroads at Cahermore. An alternative approach may be made by turning off the N 18 from Oranmore a short distance south of the turning for Ballylee Castle. A National Monument sign points the way and the road winds its way through lush meadows enclosed by broken stone walls in 'surprisingly English-looking' countryside.

Access to the castle is gained by crossing common land, rough pasture for cattle. A walk over large limestone boulders between short trees will bring the visitor up to the walls of this impressive tower house visible from the road. The walls of this old tower house are in a wonderful state of preservation but the interior is in a parlous state. It is a pity that such places were so neglected over the previous few centuries. This tower rises five levels and it has a ghost!

Today Lydacan is a National Monument so one may suppose that in the course of time some restoration work could be undertaken there. Meanwhile it remains the home of an apparition! Mention is made of it in Lady Gregory's book, Visions and Beliefs in the West of Ireland, where she refers to a description given by a local of a 'longfaced', tall ghostly woman wearing grand clothes and on her 'head something yellow and slippery' (taken to be a crown). The book also mentions of a banshee in Kinvarra which wails for the Hynes & Fahys!

The building is very similar to its cousin tower at Dunguaire but without a keep and towerlet and the roof has long since disappeared. Its base is rectangular measuring approximately 40 [12.19 metres] by 30 [9.14 metres] feet along the outside walls. It is about 60 feet [18.28 metres] high.

A stone stile has been erected in the castle doorway to keep out larger animals such as the cattle which graze nearby. Left of the doorway there is the usual small guard chamber and to the right a short passage leading to a spiral stairway. Above its only entrance is a recess, flush with the inside wall. The recess probably housed a sturdy door or portcullis. Within the entrance 'hall' and above it in the 'ceiling' there is a 'murder' hole through which defenders might have thrown spears or poured the traditional boiling oil on attackers who may have broken through the heavy door. To the right, near the entrance hall begins a spiral stone staircase constructed in the usual way to give the defenders the width of the stairs downward for right handed swordsmen and to handicap right handed attackers by giving them the narrow tread of the stairs on their right. (There is at least one castle in Ireland in which the staircase gives advantage to left-handed swordsmen since left-handedness was a characteristic of that particular family).

The lower ground floor chamber is smaller than the upper chambers because the walls at ground level are much thicker than above. In this respect Lydacan is like Dunguaire in that the walls are about 8 to 9 feet [about 2.5 metres] thick at ground level. The inside chamber itself measures about 19 feet [5.79 metres] by 20 feet [6.09 metres] and would probably have been used as a store room or stable as the inadvisability of having windows at ground level is obvious and a windowless room would have been an inconvenient place to live in. The roof of this lower room is arched and stone built.

Off the first landing up the staircase and to the left is a small room in the floor of which is the 'murder hole' referred to previously. This room was probably a guardroom but during normal occupation the murder hole would have been capped to prevent the guard from dropping through it! By climbing a few more steps up the spiral staircase visitors can enter a principal living chamber, the floor of which is arched upwards, the convex side of the lower chamber's roof. In its day this stone floor would have been laid with wooden planks of course. This room would have been the lord's main living area as it is much bigger than the lower floor where the doorkeeper only may have bedded. In this room and in the rooms above it there are fireplaces and arched recesses suitable for furniture and cupboards. A large arched recess set in the wall is a feature of this room. Above this room there have been other chambers: one of them directly above the guardroom.

At the top of all four walls there are corbels which carried some form of machicolation..That which would have been the uppermost room of all is now open to the sky and to the rooks which circle around and above the tower today. The stone flooring is still there but it is certainly in need of repair having at least one gaping hole so the Public Works Department have barred the way to visitors. This top storey in its time would have been the general living quarters with a kitchen roofed over with high-pitched timber capped by either slates or wooden shingles or thatch. As with Dunguaire there would have been a narrow walkway around the edge of the sloping roof. Today one can only glimpse the sky through iron railings!

Lydacan or Lydican Castle was a residence of the Lynch family in the 1770s. The OS Name Books record the "substantial residence of Mr. Gunning" in Lydacan in the 1830s. Lydacan Castle was purchased by Martin O'Flaherty in the mid-19th century and was subsequently sold by him to James Greated. It was burnt in 1922 and the ruins remain. Map Reference: M438080

ARDRAHAN CASTLE

About three miles away, as one of the rooks of Lydacan might fly and to the north-east are the remains of Ardrahan Castle. There is some evidence of several successive defensive works there but not much is left. All that is left of a probable 13th century castle is not much more than part of a large jagged stone keep lying to the east of the road from Clarinbridge to Gort just across the railway line near the village. Nearby is the base of a round stone tower and all sits on ground which was probably encircled by a defensive ditch and earth wall.

Some sources refer to this ruin as a Burke Castle, which indeed it was but only after its capture from the O'Heyne in 1264 A.D. The original castle was the chief residence of the lords of Aidhne until then and its capture by Walter de Burgo marks the beginning of the extension of the power of the de Burgos family in the area. The keep of the castle has been dated as 1250 Anglo-Norman. Some sources hold that the name Ardrahan is a derivative of Ard Ri hEidhne, meaning a place of the High King hEidhne whereas others say its origins lie in the term Ard Raithin, meaning a high ringfort. Certainly there are signs in the contours of the land surrounding the castle ruins of a probable ringfort and there are the remains of a round tower, one of only four such towers in Galway County but Ardrahan does not stand on a hill. The original fort was probably taken by Richard de Burgo in about 1236 when he conquered Galway and he then passed Ardrahan over to Maurice Fitzgerald.

Ardrahan was in contention some ten years previously. In the year 1212 A.D., Donnachad O'Heyne was blinded by Aodh, the son of Cathal Croihhdearg O'Conor so it is not surprising to learn that after Owen O'Heyne became chief he allied himself with the sons of King Roderic O'Conor against that very Aodh (Hugh), the son of Cathal (Charles the Red-Handed) O'Conor in 1225. The Annals of the Four Masters had this to say as reported by MacFirbis:

"...on which occasion Hugh O'Conor despatched his brother Felim and others of the chiefs of his people and a large body of English soldiers, into Hy Fiachrach Aidhne to plunder Eoghan O'Heyne, and they encamped one night at Ardrahan, for the purpose of plundering the country early the next morning; but when O'Flaherty of Iar Connaught, and the other enemies of Hugh O Conor, had heard that the English were here stationed with the intention of plundering Eoghan O'Heyne, they did not neglect their friend, but marched' with one mind and one accord', until they came to a place near Ardrahin, where they halted, and having held consultation, they came to the resolution of sending Tuathal, the sone of Muircheartach, and Taithleach O'Dowd with a strong force, to Ardrahin, while O'Flaherty and the son of Muircheartach O'Conor were to remain with their forces outside. The two O'Dowds, with their soldiers, marched courageously and boldly into the town of Ardrahin, and made a vigorous and desperate attack upon the English, whom they put to flight east and west. The party who fled eastwards were pursued by the O'Dowds, and the constable, or captain of the English received two wounds, one from the javelin of Tuathal O'Dowd and the other from that of Taithleach, which left him lifeless; but the party who fled westwards met O'Flaherty and the son of Muircheartach O'Conor, and routed them to their misfortune. After this the sons of Roderic and their supporters made peace with Hugh O'Conor and his friends, which the annalists remark was an unseasonable peace, as there was no church or territory in Connaught at the time that had not been plundered or laid waste".

THE HYNES-O'CONNOR MARRIAGE STONE

No doubt as on every other occasion, plundering would have meant a great deal of suffering being borne by the common people. At least in these times, the decision makers, the aristocracy put their lives on the line unlike in our own century when they can murder hundreds of thousands through highly mechanised weapons wielded by underlings without themselves having to fight up close and personal.

In the former Church in Wales chapel at Ardrahan there is a large marriage stone so called because it shows carved features from the husband's and wife's family coats of arms on either side. On this marriage stone, dimensions, 37" [94 cm] by 33 1/2" [85 cm] by 8 1/2" [21.5 cm], the husband's coat of arms appears on the dexter side (on the right of the knight holding the shield, that is on the left of the person facing the shield). The wife's coat of arms is on the sinister side i.e. on the left of the knight holding the shield. The motto on the Ardrahan arms is TURRIS FORTIS NOBIS DEUS, [God Our Tower of Strength]. In volume 38 of the proceedings of the Royal Society of Antiquaries Dr. Foley describes the coat of arms as that of the O'Hynes.

Marriage stone from fireplace of principal room in castle.

An interesting comparison may be made between the almost faded details of the stone shield on the viewer's left of a tomb in the O'Shaughnessy Chapel in Kilmacduagh and the beautifully clear cut details on the stone in Ardrahan some 10 miles to the north east. This stone was placed over a Hynes grave in 1777 by another Hynes who carried it by cart from the ruins of a castle, probably Ardrahan but possibly Lydacan. It was placed in the Ardrahan graveyard to mark the graves of Brian and Owen Hynes 1777(?).

A feature on the wife's arms, a stag, in all probability, represent the O'Connors of Corcomroe. The tower with lions certainly looks like O'Shaughnessy arms but the author can find no trace of an O'Shaughnessy/O'Connor connection and he finds it difficult to reconcile the altar tomb shield with the first baronet of Gort whose wife was an O'Brien and not an O'Connor. There was however a Hynes/O'Connor connection in the early 17th century, when Eugene O'Heyne of Lydacan Castle married Margarita O'Connor of Corcomroe.

CURRANROE CASTLE

A reference in the 'Four Masters' for 1599 mentions a place, near Corcomroe at the head of Aughnish Bay, called Rubha or rue-land where there was a castle surrounded by that particular herb, rue, a plant with a strong bitter odour and taste. The last of the O'Hynes living there was Peter, the son of Flan Boy O'Heynes of Kinturlough who was living in the year 1641, the last descendant of whom was mentioned by MacFirbis, John Hynes of New Quay in the Burren, a man who had "acquired a handsome property by honest industry".

However, on the 1st of November, 1755, the day of the earthquake at Lisbon, a castle on the western boundary of the parish, which belonged to the O'Heyne, was destroyed to its foundation and a portion of it swallowed up; and at the same time the chimneys and battlements of Cahirglissane, another O'Heyne castle, rocked and then fell into a chasm, which was formed by rending the rock to the depth of several fathoms.

James Frost, an historian of Clare, in his charming book, *The History and Topography of County Clare* mentioned the Hynes castle of Roo (Curranroe,

4 miles along the coast) which fell during the Lisbon earthquake of 1755. "In the townland of Ballyhehan, situate in this parish stands a castle belonging formerly to one of the O'Loghlens. Corra an Rubha also belongs to this parish and in it a castle existed which was the residence of O'Heyne, chief of the Ui Fiachrach Aidhne. That castle fell in the year 1755 at the very moment when the earthquake in Lisbon happened. The present representative of the branch of the O'Heynes who lived in this castle and also in the castle of... Ballybranaghan at Kinvara, is a descendant of John Hynes, son of James, son of John, who lived at Poulanisce, son of Brian, son of Peter, the last who is said to have lived at Curranroe Castle. The senior branch of this once powerful family was represented in 1839 by Mr. Hynes of Ardrahan, well known in the country as a process server. He was senior lineal descendant of Guaire Aidhne, King of Connaught so celebrated by the Irish bards for his hospitality".

The cause of that destruction of the castle at Roo lay in far away Portugal; in fact 1620 km or 1007 miles away! It was the Lisbon earthquake of 1755 when on all Saints' Day, November 1, at 9.40 a.m., a tremendous upheaval shook Lisbon. The principal shock waves lasted for a full six minutes. All the city's most important buildings were demolished by the violent shaking and at least 12,000 dwellings fell down. As it was a holy day most of Lisbon's citizens were attending church and many thousands of those people were crushed under falling masonry. Sixty thousand people were killed, some of them in huge 'tsunami' or shock waves from the sea and others died in fires which broke out throughout the city. The tsunami reached a height of 60 feet [18.28 metres] near Cadiz and 40 feet [12.19 metres] near Lisbon itself. The shock wave could be felt in Martinique which lay over 3700 miles [5920 km] away.

Not only was far away Roo shaken to its foundations but so too was the whole of Christendom in its tenets and beliefs as people wondered at the seeming callousness of Providence as thousands were killed whilst attending mass. All over Europe, sinners and righteous alike began to do penance for fear of further Divine retribution to come. Voltaire expressed his cynicism at the 'beneficence' of God while Jean Jacques Rousseau observed that it was just as well that natural disasters killed off a few thousands now and again.

Dunguaire was severely shaken on that day but Roo Castle actually fell, much of it swallowed up by a chasm which opened up beneath it. One has only to consider the cavernous nature of the coast near both castles to believe how easily the ground with its limestone hollows could be moved dramatically during the earthquake.

Today's curious visitor, armed with a copy of *The Burren*, a map of the uplands of north-west Clare, drawn up by T.D. Robinson can locate the very spot upon which that particular O'Heynes castle once stood, 4 miles from Kinvarra along the coast road N67 a short distance before that road crosses the road from Funshinmore and the junction with Corcair Pass. Just off the road on the sea shore a mound of grass and rock rises near a gate. The only clue to its having been a building are the chunks of cemented masonry, which lie on the mound. Like Dunguaire Castle, Roo stood on the shoreline with lookouts across the Bay; Aughnish Bay.

CAHERERILLAN CASTLE

The name appears in a number of alternative spellings: Cahererillan, Caherurlane, Cahererrellon, Cahir Irlane, Cathair Eirioláin (translates as Erilan's Stone Fort). It is an ivy- covered ruined tower house, the remains of a Hynes castle. (Visitors may find this place difficult to locate and get to across fields and a very narrow road. Its co-ordinates are: Longitude: 8° 56' 53" West; Latitude: 53° 6' 17" North

Some sources attribute this tower house, 6 floors tall, to the O'Shauhnessys and it may well have been occupied by them at some time because they were close kinsmen of the O Heyne, but O Heynes certainly did live there as attested by the following documentary evidence.

DOMINIC O'HEYNE BECOMES A SPANISH NOBLEMAN

The following is a translation of an interesting document associated with an application made by Dominic Hynes for membership of a Spanish order of nobility. The affirmation by an Irish priest, Fr. Hynes, was written in Latin and it has here been translated by Fr. James Webb, Mold, Wales:

"I, the undersigned parish priest of the parish church of Caharerrellon, In the Diocese of Duach, in the Kingdom of Ireland, in the province of Connaught, in the County of Galway and the Barony of Kiltarton, do hereby make known to all who may scrutinise this letter that I have diligently examined the baptismal registers of this parish of Cahererrellon and have found in one of them, written at the time of my predecessor, Thomas O'Grady, who was parish priest of this parish for almost sixty years, the following entry ...

"On the 4th. of August, 1683, this present, year, I baptised, according to the rites of our holy mother the Catholic, apostolic and Roman Church, the legitimate son of Edmund O' Heyne & Mistress Joan O'Shaughnessy, Gort, born in their legitimate matrimonial bed around nine o'clock in the morning.

The godparents were the nobleman Oliver Martin and Mistress Christina French of Cahercunny, both Catholic and professing the apostolic and Roman faith. He was given the name of Dominic, in testimony of which, the godparents and myself appended our signatures on the day and year above-mentioned. Mr.Oliver Martin, Mrs. Christina French, Thomas O'Grady, PP."

I have written all this out verbatim (as bound to) at Cahererrellon, and this at the request of Dominic O' Heyne and in accord with the entry In our register in the year of Our Lord, 1703.
Terence O' Heyne.

THE SUMMARY OF THE GENEALOGY OF DOMINGO O' HEYNE OF CAHERERILLAN, COUNTY GALWAY, 1683

Reads in Spanish:
Genealogia de El Capitan de Dragones Irlandes Don Domingo O Heyne, natural de Cahererrellan, pretendiente al avito de la orden de Santiago de que Su Magestad, Dios le guarde, le ha hecho merced. No ha residido en Indias.
Padres: Don Edmundo O Heyne, natural del lugar de Cahererrellan, y Dona Juana O Shasnessy, Natural de la villa de Gort.
Abuelos Paternos: don Eugenio O Heyne, natural del lugar de Leidecan, y

Dona Margarita O Conor, natural del lugar de Corcomroe.

Abuleos Maternos: don Edmundo O Shasnessy, natural del dich lugar de Gort, y Dona Maria de Burgo, natural de la villa de Ysderqueli, todas las naturalezas en el reino de Yrlanda.

Madrid y Diziembre cinco de mill setecientos y nueve.

Here is a translation by Margaret Webster of Mold, Wales.

Genealogy of Captain of the Irish Dragoons, Dominic O Heyne, native of Cahererrellan, applicant to the membership of the Order of Saint James, which favour has been extended to him by His Majesty (God Save Him). He has not served in the Indies.

Parents:

Edmund O Heyne, a native of the town of Cahererrellan and Joan O Shaughnessy, native of the town of Gort.

Paternal Grandparents:

Eugene O Heyne, a native of the town of Leidecan and Margaret O'Connor, native of Corcomroe.

Maternal Grandparents:

Edmund O Shaughnessy, native of the aforementioned town of Gort, and Maria de Burgo, of the town of Isertkelly, all inhabitants of the kingdom of Ireland.

Madrid, the 5th. Of December, 1709.

AUTHOR'S NOTES ON THE TEXT

The fact that the paternal grandparents were Eugene O Heyne, a native of Leidecan and Margaret O'Connor, native of Corcomroe, gives us the strongest clue to the origins of the marriage stone now held in the parish church of Ardrahan. The wife's side of the coat of arms shows the stag symbol of the O'Connors of Corcomroe and although the Hynes arms look like that of an O'Shaughnessy, except for the crest, an eighteenth century Hynes identified them and placed the stone on his brother's grave in 1777. Perhaps that man transported the stone all the way from this castle and no other.

Here, in these depositions, lies documentary evidence of an O' Heyne of Cahererillan married to an O'Connor of Corcomroe. Hynes and

O'Shaughnessy may have shared the same coats of arms despite the apparent differences in today's renditions.

'He has not lived in the Indies.' This phrase was included to demonstrate the fact that the claimant was an aristocrat in his own right. Spaniards living in the Indies often assumed false titles when out there and tried to pass them off a genuine once back in Spain.

These depositions included a list of notable Irishmen who as serving officers in Spanish service testified to the aristocratic background of Dominic.

The Edmund O' Heyne mentioned here must have been the one named in the will of Sir Dermot O'Shaughnessy, 1671. [See *The O'Shaughnessys* by J. P. Hynes].

Cahererrellon: There is an ivy covered ruined tower house the remains of a Hynes castle at Cahererillan, in County Galway.

Joan O' Shaughnessy of Gort, was a daughter of the chieftain from the O'Shaughnessy Castle of Gortinsegualre.

Both the Martins and the Frenchs had come out from the 'City of the Tribes', Galway. They were of Anglo-Norman descent. After the dispossession of the O' Heyne, the Martins inherited the Hynes Castle of Dunguaire.

Father Terence O Heyne: A pewter chalice, once used by this priest during penal times is now held by Mrs.Hynes-O'Connor of Poulneceann [The name means 'cave of heads'. It is said that the heads of executed priests were once thrown into it.]

There is an associated statement, in Spanish which names the Irish sponsors for Dominic.

SPONSORS FOR DOMINGO O HEYNE, MADRID, 1709

Tobias de Burgo , Knight of Santiago, Ambassador of James Ill to Spain, b.Farrantabla,Co.Limerick, Ireland

Henry Crafton ,Brigadier in Spanish service; b. Galway city, Ireland

Lucas Keogh, Lieutenant Colonel in Spanish service; b. Ireland)

Domingo Hicky, Major in Spanish service; b. Ireland

Daniel Mac Suini, Captain in Spanish service, later Colonel;
b.Co. Cork, Ireland

Juan Hely, Captain in Spanish service, later Major General; b.
Cork, Ireland

Thomas Gibbons, Captain in Spanish service; b.Leinster, Ireland

Eduardo Nangle, Adjutant Major in Spanish service; b. Ireland

Nicolas Bodquini, Franciscan; b. Galway city, Ireland

Eduardo Crean, Business agent; b. Co. Galway, Ireland

Andres Caroll, b. Sligo, Ireland

Juan Carol, Business agent; b. Galway, Ireland

Patricio de Borg, Lieutenant in Spanish service; b. Ireland

Diego Cavana, Lieutenant In Spanish service; b. Ireland

Nicholas Falon, Priest; b. Connaught, Ireland

Ricardo Duely, Priest; b. Co.Galway, Ireland

Ricardo Gorman, Priest; b. Co.Kilkenny, Ireland

Valentin Hackett, Priest; b .Kilkenny, Ireland

Juan Geraldino, Major in Spanish service; b. Ireland

Baltasar Englis, Captain in Spanish service; b. Limerick city, Ireland

It would be interesting to discover the descendants of the Wild Geese who took up service during the 16th, 17th and 18th centuries in the armies of Europe! During the Napoleonic Wars three Irish infantry regiments served in the Spanish army: They were: Irlanda (raised 1698); Hibernia (1709); and Ultonia (1709). In later years only the officers were Irish or of Irish descent whereas the soldiers were mostly Spanish. Would their surnames have changed much over the centuries?

CAHERGLASSAUN CASTLE

Like its cousin castles the name appears in a number of alternative spellings Caherglissane, Caheralussane, Cathair Ghliosain, Caherlissaan, Caherlissane, Caheralussane, Caherglassane. It is possible that it is the castle which stands on the west side of the present Caherglissane Turlough, a lake 42 hectares in size, in the south west extremity of the parish of Ardrahan, Barony of Kiltartan..5 km inland from Kinvara - Latitude : 53°

6' 14 N- Longitude: 8° 52' 27

In O'Donovan's Survey it is written "In the townland of CaherErrilanin this parish, there is a square castle in good preservation said to have been erected by O'Heyne in whose county it certainly is."

At the same time that Curran Roe castle tumbled, the chimneys and battlements of the castle at Caherglissane "...rocked and fell into a chasm several feet deep". The Clare Champion Newspaper reported that during the earthquake, "deep and yawning chasms" were carved out along the Clare coastline at Killomoran, Caherglissane, Gort and Kinvara and that a castle at Coranroe on the north coast of Clare was also destroyed.

During the 19th century lead mining was carried out near there. A mile or so from Kinvarra is a hole in the rock, called the Pigeon Hole, which leads to a natural cavern, three or four hundred feet in extent

DUNOWEN CASTLE

Dunowen is the site of an almost forgotten Hynes castle. MacFirbis mentions Aodh Buidhe (Hugh Boy) O'Heynes as the ancestor of O'Heyne of the castle of Dunowen whereas Fahey says that Eoghan Buidhe (Owen Boy) was father of the first of the Dunowen O'Heynes. Hugh was said to be one of the four sons of Flann, son of Conor O'Heyne and brother of Rory who died in 1578.

Dunowen was described by O'Donovan in Hy Fiachrach as a townland, within which lay an ancient fort, within which stood a castle, in the parish and barony of Kiltartan. The ancient fort of Dunowen was built of stone without mortar running along the edge of a precipitous crag rising steeply from the lakes which surrounded, east and west. Those ancient earthworks predated the castle which according to Fahey stood to the westward side. Could this fort be the Nastaig Fort as shown on the Ordnance Survey map of the district? If so, then the castle on the edge of Caherglissane Lake is 'Dunowen'. On the other hand, the castle which lies just north of the road running east and west through Owenbristy could actually be the Castle of Dunowen.

The Flower of Ballylee, Máire Ní hEidhin, Mary Hynes

Ballylee Castle

A few miles to the north of Gort Inse Guaire lies the entrance to Coole Park where stood the home of Augusta Lady Gregory. She, a famous lady of letters, took a leading part in the 19th and 20th Century revival of Irish literature and drama in the company of W.B. Yeats, St. John Gogarty and others. She and they helped found the famous Abbey Theatre in Dublin. Yeats once told the poet John Masefield Coole that Park was the most beautiful place in the world. When thinking about that it should not be forgotten that the beautiful ancient parkland of Coole lay within the Hynes/O'Shaughnessy septs other beautiful territories!

Lady Gregory was born into one of the families which arrived in Ireland in Cromwell's time. Descended from Augusta Persse (of the Percy family of Northumberland) she was born in Roxborough House on the Loughrea Road. Her birthplace was burned down during the Irish Civil War and it was probably one of the great houses which Yeats referred to when he described the havoc caused in the district during the conflict.

Within the grounds of Coole Park may be seen the famous 'signature tree' upon which many of the literary figures of the clay carved their initials while visiting Lady Gregory. There, with patience, may be deciphered the initials of: GB. Shaw, Sean O'Casey, Jack and William Yeats, J. M. Synge, Augustus John etc

After the death of her husband Sir William Gregory of Coole House, Lady Gregory devoted her time and energy to travelling around the barony of Kiltartan collecting folklore which she used in her plays and prose. In her play Colman and Guaire those two leading historical characters of the Ui Fiachrach Aidhne appear. They also have parts a play Kincora first performed at the Abbey Theatre in 1905 about another episode of Irish history. For example, in Kincora, Brian Boru is seen to emerge from his tent at Clontarf, just as the Danes are retreating to the sea where they must make their last stand. Brian's servant assures his master that Malachi is safe whereupon Brian predicts that Malachi will outlive them all.Brennan, the servant, reports upon the progress of the battle by saying: "O'Hynes and the men of Connacht are doing great deeds. There are no traitors among us but the men of Meath."

Both Lady Gregory and Yeats echo the past glories of the Ui Fiachrach Aidhne in their own fascination with the beautiful Mary Hynes, the miller's daughter from Ballylee. Mary Hynes had been immortalised by the poet Antoine O'Reachtabra (Blind Raftery). His poem of adulation tells of how he met Mary Hynes as he was going to Mass on a wet and windy day and after 'seeing' her by the cross at Kiltartan he fell madly in love with her, as did most people!

Raftery tells how he politely greeted the beautiful Mary as he knew her to be a kind and gentle woman. She invited him to her home in Ballylee and he walked rapturously with her across the fields. At table she invited him to drink a glass or two with her. Raftery sings her praise:
"O star of light and O sun in harvest; O amber hair, O my share of the world! Will you come with me on the Sunday, till we agree together before all the people?"

Raftery promises her song every Sunday evening with punch or wine on the table. He celebrates the sweetness of the air on the hill wherever she walks, whenever she picks blackberries and nuts. The very birds make music for her and the ghostly music of the Sidhe may be heard.

"What is the worth of greatness till you have the light of the flower of the branch that is by your side? There is no good to deny it or try to hide it; she is the sun in the heavens who wounded my heart. There was no part in Ireland I did not travel, from the rivers to the tops of the mountains; to the edge of Lough Greine whose mouth is hidden, and I saw no beauty hut was behind hers. Her hair was shining and her brows were shining too; her face was like herself her mouth pleasant and sweet; She is the pride and I give her the branch; she is the shining flower of Ballylee. It is Mary Hynes, the calm and easy woman, has beauty in her mind and in her face. If a hundred clerks were gathered together, they could not write down half her ways." (From Lady Gregory's *Kiltartan History Book,* a fascinating book which can be recommended for further reading on the barony of Kiltartan,).

Lady Gregory recalled that she had spoken to an old woman who had known Mary Hynes and who said of her "The sun and the moon never shone upon anything so handsome". The old lady had then gone on to recite Raftery's song of praise – *The Pearl that was in Ballylee* a song that has travelled the world with the Irish.

There is a version of the poem in the Faber Book of Irish Verse but for some reason the name has been changed to Mary Egan! On one of Yeats's visits to Ballylee before he actually bought the castle, he wrote: 'There is an old square castle, Ballylee, inhabited by a farmer and his wife, and a cottage where a daughter and son-in-law live and a little mill with an old miller and old ash trees throwing green shadows upon a little river and great stepping stones. I went there two or three times last year to talk to the miller about Biddy Early, a wise woman that lived in Clare some years ago, and about her saying there is a cure for all evil between the two mill wheels of Ballylee and to find out from him or another whether she meant the moss between the running waters or some other herb. I have been there this summer and I shall be there again before it is autumn, because Mary Hynes, a beautiful woman whose name is still a wonder by turf fires, died there sixty years ago, for our feet would linger where beauty has lived its life of sorrow to make us understand that it is not of this world'.

As this visit was made in 1896, Mary Hynes must have died in Ballylee in 1836.

Yeats bought the castle and its adjoining cottage in 1916 for 35 pounds and came to love his Ballylee, once the dwelling of Ulick de Burgo in 1597 and of Richard de Burgo in 1617.

Further adulation by Yeats appears in The Tower, where he celebrates the local memory of Mary Hynes in his lines:

Some few remembered still when I was young
A peasant girl commended by a song,
Who'd lived somewhere upon that rocky place
And praised the colour of her face,
And had the greater joy in praising her,
Remembering that, if walked she there,
Farmers jostled at the fair
So great a glory did the song confer.

And certain men, being maddened by those rhymes
Or else by toasting her a score of times,
Rose from the table and declared it right
To test their fancy by their sight;
But they mistook the brightness of the moon
For the prosaic lightAnd one was drowned in the great bog of Cloone.

Yeats also took Mary's lineal ancestor, Guaire, as the subject of a play, *The King's Threshold* but in his version Senchan becomes the 'hero' who fasts to death against the King of Connaught.

After Yeats's death, the castle at Thoor Ballylee fell into a ruinous state until restoration at the hands of the Kiltartan Society and the Bord Failte, the Irish Tourist Board. The Kiltartan Society, founded in 1961 by Mrs. Mary Hanley, advised the Board who funded the project. Restoration work was helped along by the drawings made by Professor Scott and photographs taken by a local photographer, Thomas Hynes, during his visit to the tower in 1926. (His photographs were donated by Miss Mary Hynes of Dungory, Kinvara.) Today's visitor to Thoor Ballylee will find it a delightful place where one can sense the past glories of the ancient de Burgos and the Ui Fiachrach Aidhne. There, too, can be sensed the presence of the poet who like Lady Gregory and so many others fell in love with the people and the atmosphere of the ancient territory of the Gaelic chieftains. The road to Ballylee is well marked from the N18 Gort to Oranmore road.

BLIND RAFTERY

Raftery's grave lay neglected and half-forgotten for many years, but it has since been carefully restored and well marked by the Public Works Department. It may be reached from the N 18. If travelling from Oranmore south, the motorist may turn left near the crossroads where the road to the right, westwards, is marked for Kinvarra and Aillwee Cave. Close to the turn-off may be found a traditional Irish pub called 'Raftery's Rest' Kilcolgan, serving the ubiquitous draught Guinness. The road to the 'Cemetery of the Poets' (Reilig Na Bhfili) is marked for Killineen Graveyard.

A new headstone has been placed over Raftery and nearby the graves of the poet brothers Mark and Patsy Callanan. 'Blind Raftery' was buried on St. Stephen's Night in 1835 when a lively breeze blew through the graveyard. A plain wooden coffin was lowered into the grave and, although the wind blew strongly, almost miraculously, the naked flames of two candles held by the handful of mourners never wavered but remained alight like the dead poets songs and ballads!

A curious account appears in Lady Gregory's Kiltartan History Book which is intriguing in its brevity, suggesting an exciting tale which we may never know in full:
"Corly, that burned his house in the Burren, was very bad, and it was O'Connell brought him to the gallows. The only case O Connell lost was against the MacNamaras, and he told them he would be even with them, and so when Corly, that was a friend of theirs, was brought up he kept his word. There was no doubt about him burning the house, it was to implicate the Hynes he did it, to lay it on them. There was a girl used to go out milking at daybreak and she awoke and the moon was shining, and she thought it was day, and got up and looked out, and she saw him doing it". Here Lady Gregory is reporting the anecdote which had been told her in Kiltartanese.

The O'Shaughnessy Chieftains

Gort Inse Guaire 'the holm field of Guaire', County Galway, has been described in the past as a tidy town. Thackeray said of it, that it, "… looked as if it had wondered how the deuce it got itself in the midst of such desolate country, and seemed to bore itself there considerably. It had nothing to do and no society." At the time, Gort was having a hard time of it, as indeed was most of Ireland. In fact a few years later one lady traveller said that she had gone from door to door in the town asking for bread only to be told, "The people of Gort don't eat, ma'am, we have no bread".

The west of Ireland was said to have the most enervating climate in Western Europe. Its blandness and narrow range of seasonal variation led McAlister to remark that to this quite irredeemable vice of the Irish climate is due to the notorious fact that Irishmen always do better in any country other than their own! This is perhaps only sardonic comment, as the fact of the matter was that many Irishmen were forced by circumstances, well out of their control, to seek their fortunes abroad to escape the stifling penal laws. Among the many thousands who left Ireland during the 17th, 18th and 19th Centuries were the descendants of Guaire: the Hynes, the O'Shaughnessys, the O'Clearys, the Killikellys, the O'Cahills and the O'Cahans and others.

Of the O'Shaughnessys, some historians suggest that were not descended directly from Guaire but from Guaire's brother, Aodh. Both brothers had Colman as their father. This is an unlikely event as most evidence points to Guaire as their direct forebear.

The O'Shaughnessys' territory was called Kinel Aedha na Echtghe and the people were said to be of the tribe of Aodh. They were associated with the mountain Sliabh Echtghe (Slieve Aughty) and they lived in the eastern half of the diocese of Kilmacduagh. Both O'Clery and Keating, in the Great Book of Lecan, Leabhar (Mór) Leacain, a medieval transcript, attribute their descent from Guaire and as his descendants they were a major sept of the Ui Fiachrach Aidhne taking their name from Seachnasach who was chief of the sept in the year 1100. Their ancestors could be traced back to King Daithi, the last pagan king of Ireland.

The O'Shaughnessys' main stronghold was in Gort during the Middle Ages. It was built on the site of Guaire's second palace but today there is nothing left of this castle except for some masonry incorporated in the buildings behind Keane's store. This was the stronghold in which Sir Dermot O'Shaughnessy lived after his great great grandfather who had forsaken the Gaelic order for 'surrender and regrant', and joined the Federation of Kilkenny.

O'SHAUGHNESSY ACCEPTS A KNIGHTHOOD FROM HENRY THE EIGHTH

The political power of many of the Irish chieftains began to decline during the reign of King Henry the Eighth of England when they refused to surrender their lands on a "grant regrant" basis. We are told by Monsignor Fahey that the O'Heynes refused proffered English titles at this time keeping the old Gaelic title of "The O'Heynes".

In 1533, King Henry wrote, "We have made MacNamarow, O'Shagness and Denis Grady, Knights". His letter went on to say that, in return, the named chieftains had to repudiate their old titles accepting their lands instead from the Crown. Letters patent dated 3 December 1543, granted Sir Dermot O'Shaughnessy, knight, captain of his nation, in consideration of his submission "… all the manors, lordships, towns and townlands of Gortinchegory which lands the said Sir Dermot and his ancestors had unjustly possessed against the crown". An ecclesiastical dignity was promised to a Malachy Donohoo (Donaghue) and a bishopric, of Kilmacduagh to William O'Shaughnessy, possibly a fictitious son. (In fact an actual son. See *The O'Shaughnessys* by J.P. Hynes.) . The critical word in that document was 'submission' , this chieftain and others had given over their peoples' land and freedom to another. His action was another marker for the end of the Gaelic order where land weas held in trust for the whole clan.

It must be said in O'Shaughnessy's favour that although he surrendered to Henry he did not give up his old faith as some of the other chieftains did at that time. On 12 July 1559, the Lord Deputy of England could have been seen dining at O'Shaughnessy's castle in Gort, served with the Guaire hospitality which the O'Shaughnessys practised throughout the centuries. No doubt the Lord Deputy was charmed by the beauty and accomplishments of Lady O'Shaughnessy, formerly the Lady Mor O'Brien.

The two sons of this O'Shaughnessy were Roger, who eventually succeeded to the title and lands, and Dermot, the Swarthy, who travelled to England, to court, in service to the Earl of Leicester, Robert Dudley, a favourite of the new Protestant Queen of England, Elizabeth. Dermot brought a great deal of trouble with him on return to Ireland.

In 1565, the venerable Primate Creagh, a champion of the "old faith" had been imprisoned in the Tower of London but had managed to escape, as did only one or two others in the history of that fortress. Believing himself safe in the territories of the O'Shaughnessy chiefs, the Bishop had sought refuge there, but Dermot's loyalties were to the English Crown so he had the Primate re-arrested. For this ignominious deed Dermot earned the contempt of his kinsmen and the gratitude of the Queen.

Queen Elizabeth's letter to this traitorous O'Shaughnessy read: "Right trusty and well-beloved, we greet thee well. 'As well by sundry advertisements from our right trusty and well-beloved Sir H. Sydney, our Deputy in that our realm of Ireland, as also by our own demonstrations, we have right well understood and perceived your good will and disposition to serve and obey us. Whereof as we cannot he unmindful, so among other things we will not forget to allow right well of your service, staying and bringing to our said Deputy an unloyal subject of that land, being a feigned bishop, who not long before broke out of the Tower of London: all which your doings and good services confirming in us more and more right good opinion of your loyalty towards us, we do so retain in our remembrance, as we will not forget the same towards you, to your comfort in any reasonable cause to be brought befóre us; and for that we understand and see your service meet to be by us allowed. We pray you to continue the same, as the occasion shall serve, by the direction of our Lord Deputy who both doth make good account of you, and testifieth the same from time to time unto us.'

DERMOT THE SWARTHY GAINS THE INHERITANCE

It was not long before Dermot availed himself of the promise of "comfort in any reasonable cause". Dermot's brother, the elder, had incautiously allied himself with the Lady Honora, daughter of Murrough O'Brien, Earl of Thomand. Honora was a professed nun and mother superior of the Augustinian monastery of Kilowen which had been seized by her father together with its lands in the tradition of the English seizures of monastic lands. Lady Honora had supposedly reneged on her vows.

Three children were born to the couple before marriage: John, Joan and Margaret were illegitimate. After marriage, 'by dispensation from Rome', William, Fergananim and Dermot were born. After the death of Sir Roger in 1569, John, the illegitimate son, took up the inheritance only to be challenged by his uncle, Dermot the Swarthy.

Dermot left the Earl's service and travelled back to Ireland to claim the inheritance. He bore a letter from the Queen; it was addressed to the Lord Deputy. "Right trusty and well beloved, we greet you well. Where on Darby O'Shaghnes, the youngest son as he saith of William O'Shaughnessy*, Lord of Kynally, in that or Realme of Ireland, hath by the means of his Lord and Master, or Coosen the Erle of Leicester, humbly required us not only to give him leave to returne to his country, but also to recommend his peticion into yow, for some order to be taken with hym upon the death of his brother, Roger O'Shagness, as being next heire unto him, we being duly informed of his honest demeaner here, and of his earnest to serve us, have been content to accompt him to or service, and do require yow to have favourable consideracion of his suite, and as you shall find it meet to place and settle him in the foresaid country, so the rather to incurrage him to persever in his fidelitie to showe him as much favor as may accord with the good government of the same contry.

Given under our signet, at or Mannor of Oteland, the 23rd of June 1570, in the 22nd year of our Reigne."

Poor John was disqualified on the grounds of his illegitimacy and Dermot took over.

---

* An error apparently. Dermot was the grandson of William O'Shaughnessy.

Ardamullivan Castle
And a Duel to the Death

In 1573, the "Queen's O'Shaughnessy", together with Ulick, son of the Earl of Clanricarde, slew Murrough O'Brien, the third Earl of Thomond. However, John, the brother of O'Brien revenged himself by driving Dermot from the ancestral home at Gort. Dermot fled to Ardameelavane Castle, another of the O'Shaughnessy strongholds. (This tower house, the O'Shaughnessey's old stronghold at Ardamullivan, built in 1567, has recently been beautifully restored and is now a National Monument.) Six years later, Dermot laid a trap for a nephew, William O'Shaughnessy, a legitimate claimant to the estate and a man favoured by the local population. William was lured to the Castle of Ardameelavane by a promise made by his uncle Dermot to engage in peaceable discussion.

On the rough ground close to the castle walls, on the southern side, Dermot attacked his nephew with all the skill he had acquired as a swashbuckling follower of Leicester in the court of England. It was to be a fight to the death. Dermot was a competent experienced swordsman who had no doubts about his ability to despatch his irritating nephew. But it did not prove easy for him. Despite the years of practice in Leicester's bodyguard, Dermot found William a well-matched opponent. William fought with the vigour of youth and the determination of the just. They fought with fierce intensity but William was run through and fell mortally wounded but so too did Dermot for he too had been severely injured during the duel. Uncle survived nephew by a mere half-hour. It is no wonder that the place of the duel is thought to be haunted by the spirits of these tragic O'Shaughnessys!

After the deaths of the two rivals, John, the illegitimate O'Shaughnessy, laid claim only to be opposed by his younger brother Dermot who was legitimate. The claimants attended a Parliament on 26 April 1585 to redress their grievances. Strange to say, although the Parliament seems to have taken no action in the case nothing more was heard of John's claim thereafter and Dermot the younger inherited. He possessed them until his death in 1606. An Indenture of Composition in 1585 has a mention:"There belong to the heires of Sir Darby O'Shahness, Knight, 101 quarters in the barony of Kiltaraghe."

SIR ROGER O'SHAUGHNESSY

A few years later, Redmond Burke supporting the Desmond League
"...traversed and plundered, and burned the country from Leitrim to
Ardameelavane, and as far as the gate of Fedane, in the west of Kinelea."
Fedane (Fiddaune) was also an O'Shaughnessy castle, built by Sir Roger.
It lies 2 miles south-west of Ardameelavane and it has a wonderful bawn,
surrounding defensive wall. (See, *The O'Shaughnessys* by James P. Hynes)

In 1615, a claim to the lands of Cappafennell and Capparell held by the
O'Shaughnessys was lodged with the Irish Court of Chancery by Fulk
Comerford. The claim arose out of a promise made by the illegitimate
John O'Shaughnessy during the dispute with his relatives in 1603. In that
year, John granted those lands to Sir Jeoffrey Fenton on condition that
Fenton frustrated Dermot O'Shaughnessy's claim to the lands in question.

Some venerable interested parties were present at the hearings: the sister-
in-law of O'Shaughnessy, Margaret, the Countess Dowager of Claricarde,
aged 80, Richard Burke, 64 years, Manus Ward, Dean of Kilmacduagh, 80,
Sir Tirrelac O'Brien and the aged Knougher (Connor) Crone O'Heyne
who lived to be over 100 years of age. The results of the appeal must be
left to speculation.

This Sir Roger O'Shaughnessy, Ruaidhrí Gilla Dubh Ó Seachnasaigh, died
in the year 1659. According to Fahey there was a portrait of the gentleman,
clothed in armour, still to be seen in Ormond Castle, Kilkenny, at the turn
of the last century. Sir Roger's coat of arms is apparent on a letter he wrote
from Fiddane Castle. They were described as 'a tower crenelled in pale
between two lions combatant with the crest an arm embowed holding a
spear'.

During the seventeenth century the O'Heynes, Kilkellys and de Burgos
had all but disappeared from the history books but the O'Shaughnessys
soldiered on, quite literally, for they continued their traditional skill at arms.
After the inevitable confiscation the O'Shaughnessys served abroad with
the French.

Sir Roger became involved, in 1635, with the Galway jurors in opposing the Wentworth scheme of land seizures. Success for Wentworth depended very much upon the intimidation of juries but the Galway jurors were not giving in to the bullying. The Stuarts then held the throne in Britain and the Irish had supposed they would get a just remedy under the new parliament but it did not turn out that way. The oppression of the Irish Catholics continued as viciously as ever.

Wentworth's *Commission of Inquiry into Defective Titles* saw to that. The Commission required the title of each deed to be questioned and declared defective unless supported by deeds preserved and registered in the Record Office, Dublin. [This process looks very like the system used by the current Israeli government to seize Palestinian lands!] Although £3000 had been paid by the proprietary of the province, registration had been neglected. This was well known by Wentworth and his commission but the idea was the dispossession of the Irish Catholics in favour of English Protestant planters. Jurors in the north of Ireland had either been bribed or co-erced into favouring the latter but the Galway jurors obstinately refused to find against the Catholics.

Wentworth had the sheriff and jurors arrested and imprisoned in Dublin. The sheriff was fined £1000 and the jurors £4000 each. They would be kept in jail until the fines were paid. As it happened the sheriff died in prison while the jurors were tortured, were pilloried with loss of ears, bored through their tongues and marked on their foreheads with hot irons.

Sir Roger O'Shaughnessy, Martin and Darcy sought and arranged an audience with the King in London to plead for the imprisoned men. Wentworth's agents intercepted them and had them arrested. Martin was kept in London, while the other two were imprisoned and fined. Their pleas never reached the King's ear, not that is until the Earl of Clanricarde managed to obtain their freedom with reduced fines. Soon afterwards the discredited Wentworth was recalled from Ireland and deprived of office.

Dermot O'Shaughnessy joined the Confederation and worked for that cause. On Sunday, 17 October 1645, Sir Charles Coote and his men surprised and slew the venerable Archbishop O'Queely. Majors W. O'Shaughnessy and Richard Burke together with Lieutenant O'Heyne, officers in the archbishop's forces were made prisoner on that occasion.

Many Irish Royalists exiled themselves to join the uncrowned King Charles abroad. Others stayed to continue the struggle and to become more and more impoverished as the years went by. The Bishop of Killala on visiting Gort Castle was proffered the traditional lavish hospitality by O'Shaughnessy but the good bishop declined the gifts as he pitied his host along with other nobles "…whose fortunes and reverses had sustained considerable diminution, and he knew right well they could not afford to indulge in the customs of other times".

The Marquis of Clanricarde wrote in the most praiseworthy terms of the service rendered by Sir Roger O'Shaughnessy, then holding a captain's commission in the King's troops. William, Roger's brother, was an officer in Clanricarde's levy and in 1648 the Corporation of Galway noted that: "Lieutenant Colonel William O'Shaughnessy, in consideration of his alliance in blood to the whole town, and for the consideration that he and his family do bear to it, and his posterity shall be hereafter free of their guild".

Gort Castle Captured By Cromwellians

Sir Roger died in the year 1659 and his son Dermot succeeded. Sir Dermot raised a troop of 50 men in Claricarde's regiment. In 1651 while Sir Dermot and his most experienced men were helping in the defence of Galway, Gort Castle was left in the care of some tenants with a small detachment of soldiers under the command of an English officer called Foliot.

Ludlow, one of the most active of Cromwell's supporters, who had been in Ireland since 1651 decided then to attack Gort Castle. The castle stood on an island in the Cannahowna or Gort River protected on the eastern side by the river where the current was often deep and strong. A bawn or outer wall some 12 feet high protected the other sides. Ludlow had no cannon so his soldiers stormed the walls using scaling ladders. Despite the small numbers of defenders Foliot afforded a spirited resistance.

The well directed fire of the attackers drove the defenders from the lower rooms of the castle. Then, the Cromwellians gained entry through a window on the ground floor. Foliot attacked them, sword in hand but was overcome by numbers and killed. Everything inflammable was set alight forcing the inhabitants to sue for mercy as many of them were women and children. Ludlow admitted that: "…being pressed by his officers that some of the principal of them might be punished with death for their obstinacy, he consented to their demands." Gilbert's publications on the Cromwellian campaigns had this to say:"After a long and great dispute about forty of the rebels were slain in the storm, and after forty were shot, the castle was burnt, but the house preserved".

Fahey, wrote that there were eighty in all, in the castle, together with women and children so one may suppose that the defenceless, also called rebels were all slain on that occasion too!

It was the callous Ludlow who said of the Burren in County Clare during his land grabbing murderous operations there in 1651-52; "It is a country where there is not enough water to drown a man, wood enough to hang one, nor earth enough to bury him."

John Prendergast in his book the 'Cromwellian Setllement of Ireland, 1868 ' said of the 1653 Act that its objective was rather to extinguish a nation than to suppress a religion , they seized the lands of the Irish , and transferred them (and with them all the power of the state) to an overwhelming flood of new English settlers, filled with the intensest national and religious hatred of the Irish." Conquerors ever, set about hating the vanquished inventing reasons to oppress them to justify their own reprehensible actions.

THE O'SHAUGHNESSYS LOSE THEIR LANDS

Following the Restoration of Charles II in 1660, the Protestants who had resisted Cromwell were quickly restored but little comfort came the way of the Catholics. Confiscations had been so widespread that even the O'Shaughnessys regained only 2000 acres of land together with his castle. The O'Shaughnessy died in 1673 and his will dated 1671 is an interesting social commentary on the times for: he asks that his remains should be laid in the ancestral tomb at Kilmacduagh; that his son should have ' five hundred and fówer score Masses to be said or celebrated for my soule immediately after my death': that the younger son should have a mortgage and some stock; that the eldest should have all the plate and household "stuffe"; that the youngest son should also have the stuffe coat with gold buttons and his rapier'. A piece of grey frieze went to Edmond O'Heyne and some grey broadcloth to Father J. Molony. James Devenisse was to have a gold diamond ring on condition he said one hundred rosaries for the dead O'Shaughnessy. Other bequests were made to the Dominicans and Augustinians of Galway.

On the succession of James II to the English throne in 1685. Catholics in both Ireland and England expected a considerable relaxation in penal laws. Subsequently after that unfortunate King's exile from England and his landing in Ireland, many of the old chieftains rallied to his help. The ensuing battles represented the chieftains' final efforts for freedom but their days were already numbered.

Sir Roger O'Shaughnessy fought at the Battle of the Boyne as a captain in the regiment of Lord Clare, his father-in-law, fighting for James II, and he died a year or two later of a broken heart, bitterly disappointed with the way things had turned out. (The relics of St. Colman had accompanied the men of Kinel Aedh at Boyne and Aughrim so it is possible the girdle was 'lost' at one of those places.)

Within ten years of those battles the O'Shaughnessy estates were confiscated by an Act of Attainder and Forfeiture issued against Sir Roger O'Shaughnessy, deceased, and his son William. An Inquisition held in the eighth year of the reign of William III mentions the residences and land lost. The Williamites passed on the confiscated estates to Irish born Thomas Prendergast who on the 15 July 1699 was created a baronet, of Gort. The grant included O'Shaughnessy's real and personal estate. Prendergast acquired the lands dishonourably by acting as an informer. He had been induced by King William to inform on his co-conspirators in an 'assassination' plot to ambush the King's coach at Turnham Green hence his reward of O'Shaughnessy lands: the greater the informer, the greater the reward. Five conspirators were executed but Prendergast was rewarded by receiving the O'Shaughnessy holdings: Lough Cutra and Gortinsguaire. William O'Shaughnessy went into exile leaving the land of his ancestors forever to serve the French.

THE CHEVALIER O'SHAUGHNESSY

In 1689, William, a boy of fifteen, began his military career as a captain of 100 men. In 1690 he was sent to France and in 1691 he was commissioned by Louis XIV, King of France, the Sun King. That same year he served at the siege of Montmelian. His military career thereafter was as follows: 1692 with the French army in Italy; 1693 at Marsaglia in Piedmont; 1696, made a company commander in Regiment at Valenza; 1697 with the army of the Meuse; 1698 captain of Grenadiers; 1701 and 1702 with the army of Germany; 1703 in battles at Kehl, Munderkingen, Hochstedt; 1794 at Blenhaim; 1705 Moselle; 1706 Ramillies; became lieutenant colonel after death of John O'Carroll; 1707 Flanders; 1708 Oudenard; 1709 Malplaquet; 1711 Arleux; 1712 Denain, Douay, Quesnay, Bouchain, Friburg; 1734 Ellingen, Philipsburg made marechal de camp; 1745 Clausen; 1742 commanded at Cambrai appointed to command at Gravelines died without issue in 1744, 2 January, aged 70 years.

Although William married Maire Jacqueline Francoise de Gauville on 15 February 1729 at Aire-sur-la Lys, they had no children. His uncle, Charles O'Shaughnessy of Ardameelavane Castle became titular head of the family. His children were Joseph, Coleman and Roebuck and after the death of the eldest, Joseph, Coleman, who became Bishop of Ossory succeeded. Coleman had served abroad as a soldier but later became a priest. In 1744 he became a legal claimant for the estates and immediately instituted a suit against Sir Thomas Prendergast, the son of Thomas. Bishop O'Shaughnessy died before 1749 at Gowran in the parish of Father John O'Heyne so Roebuck took over the claim.

He went on to take forcible possession of the family mansion at Gort when Joseph, his friends and relations, marched on the old mansion in 1749. On that occasion the troop of cavalry soldiers stationed there, preferred discretion to valour so they fled leaving Sir Joseph in possession of his ancestral hall!

The bells of Anthenry and Galway rang out for joy welcoming the return of the old line of Guaire. A poor relative, James O'Shaughnessy composed a special poem for the occasion but O'Shaughnessy had totally prejudiced his chances in the courts of law. John Prendergast-Smyth, successor to the estates filed against O'Shaughnessy at Chancery. O'Shaughnessy lost the property once and forever.

Over the years the costs of litigation had consumed a great deal of money. O'Shaughnessy received financial backing from impoverished relatives whereas Prendergast-Smyth was munificently backed by a sum of £8000 to £20,000, nobody is sure which, from Lord Brougham, Baron Brougham and Vaux. Sir Joseph died in 1785 without issue thus this line of the family which descended from Sir Dermot, knighted by Henry Tudor, passed out of history on the male side.

The old castle and mansion were demolished and a military barracks was built from the stones but that too has now disappeared. John Prendergast-Smyth, 1742 – 23 May 1817, became Lord Kiltartan, 1st Viscount Gort having no children of his own, his successor, his nephew completed the castle at Lough Cutra. This nephew was Vereker, Viscount Gort.

By 1752, a barracks had been set up in the old mansion house of the O'Shaughnessys within the walls of the former castle. In 1787, Mr. Prendergast-Smyth owned Gort and its environs as 'lord of the soil'. He is said to have let the barracks go to ruin despite the fact that the government paid him 60 pounds a year for their use. During the year 1846, the barracks accommodated 8 officers, 88 men and 116 horses and in 1856 a Captain Trotman was barrack master there. Today there is no sign of the former castle and barracks nor of the old palace of Guaire but local people believe that the site of these old buildings must have been where the river curves at the entrance of the town.

Other eminent descendants of the Kiltartan O'Shaughnessys included 'Big John' O'Shaughnessy (Sir John), 1818-1883, who became a distinguished Australian statesman and ever an ardent Catholic. Sir William Brooke O'Shaughnessy, 1809-1883, became an eminent surgeon and a pioneer of the telegraph while another branch of the family changed their name to Sandys. More about this eminent Irish family can be read in *The O'Shaughnessys* by James P. Hynes and in *The O'Shaughnessys of Muster* by John P.M. Feheney.

O 'Shaughnessy Castles

Some five miles south of Gort are the ruins of Ardamullivan Castle which was first mentioned in 1567 when Dermot, 'the Swarthy' O'Shaughnessy lay claim to it after the death of his brother, Sir Roger. Dermot, who was under the protection of Queen Elizabeth I, had betrayed Dr. Creagh, the Archbishop of Armagh, so the local people favoured the claim of Dermot's nephew, John. These two fought a duel to decide possession of the castle in 1579 while William O'Shaughnessy had taken custody of the castle. The two antagonists managed to kill each other so that neither succeeded to the inheritance.

The tower of Ardamullivan Castle, Ard-Maoldubhain, Maoldubhan's height, has five storeys with vaulting over the ground floor and over the third storey. There are carved floral motifs on the window of the top floor. After the fall of the O'Shaughnessys this abandoned castle fell into a ruinous state until minor repairs were made under the direction of Viscount Gough, in 1900. Following that it again suffered serious deterioration. During very recent restoration traces of medieval murals were found and painstakingly restored by experts. Please see the book, *The O'Shaughnessys* for more on this castle and on Fiddaun.

FIDDAUN CASTLE

Five miles south of Gort in a slightly different direction, off a minor road, which passes the L55 and the N18 near the village of Curtaun lies another O'Shaughnessy Castle, Fiddaun, Fiodh Duin - wood of the fort. It is a 16th Century tower house with six storeys set between two lakes, Lough Doo and Lough Aslaun located 13 km from Corofin on the Gort road and right, just beyond Lough Bunny and over the Galway border. When visiting please seek permission from the Forde family upon whose land it lies.

The six-sided bawn is the best preserved in the country. The

O'Shaughnessys built Fiddaun in 1574 and continued to live there until 1697 when it was confiscated. Its owner, Sir William O'Shaughnessy left Ireland for France. The widow of a Roger O'Shaughnessy re-married , becoming Helena O' Kelly and she died at Fiddaun in 1729. The castle stayed in the hands of the O'Kellys for some time after her death; probably until 1761.

Few people named O'Shaughnessy live in the area but there is a townland near Gort which commemorates the old name, Laughtyshaughnessy.

THE O'CLEARYS CLARKES, CLERKINS, MACCLEARYS, MCALARYS

The O'Clearys too are direct descendants of King Guaire Aidhne. Guaire had three sons: Nar, who was ancestor of the O'Moghans, who were for a short period lords of Aidhne; Arthgal, who was ancestor of the O'Clerys, O'Heynes and Mac Gilla Kellys; and Aoedh, ancestor of the O'Shaughnessys. Arthgal's son, Feargal was King of Connaught for a short time. Commascach was great grandson of King Feargal and his son Conchobar died in 763 A.D. A second son of Feargal, Flaitnia, was slain in the year 768. Cleireach or Cleirigh, about A.D. 850 , seventh in descent from Guaire, was grandson of Comasach and founder of the O'Cleary family who were chieftains until the close of the tenth century. Cleirigh had two sons: Maelfavail and Eidhin who was the direct ancestor of the O'Heynes who held the lordship for so long after the O'Clearys and the Kilkellys.

Maelfavail's son, Tighernach, became chief and died in the year 916 when he was followed by Maelmacduagh (a name which meant consecrated to MacDuagh). He was slain by Danes in the year 920. Flan, brother of Tighernach succeeded as king but was slain by the men of Munster in the year 950 A.D.

In the year 950 A.D. "Flann Ua Cleirigh, Lord of South Connaught, and royal heir to all Connaught, was slain by the men of Munster. Flann's son, Comhaltan, became an eminent warrior, who in the year 964, defeated Feargal O'Ruarc, King of Connaught. Some seven hundred were slain in that battle. Comhaltan died in the year 976 and Muireadhach Ua Cleirigh succeeded as Lord of Aidhne.

In 992 the son of Comhaltan, Giolla Ceallaigh O'Clery slew the son of the chief of South Connaught in battle and in 998 he slew Diarmuid, son of the chief of the O'Maddens, but in 1003 he himself was killed by Taog O'Kelly in battle. That Gioola Ceallaigh was the progenitor of the Kilkellys or Killikellys.

The last O'Cleary to hold the Lordship of Aidhne was Braon O'Clery who died in 1033. O'Clearys is one of the oldest surnames in Europe, as it was in accepted use in the 10th Century long before traditional surnames had begun. After the Anglo-Norman invasion and under pressure from their cousins the O'Shaughnessys, the O'Clerys were forced out of the Ui Fiachrach Aidhne by the de Burgos after they had made Clanrickarde their own. The O'Heynes and O'Shaughnessys stayed but had to pay chief rent to MacWilliam Oughter as his vassals, The O'Clerys settled in Donegal and Derry. The expulsion of the O'Clearys happened shortly after the fall of the O'Heyne castle at Ardrahan. The probable date was 1063 in the time of Domhnall Ua Cleirigh.

In Mayo the O'Clerys were to be found in Tirawley, west of the Moy estuary and some went on from there into Donegal becoming poets and chroniclers of the O'Donnells. The O'Clearys were given lands there and their chief seat was to be found near Ballyshannon.

Domhnall O Cleary had four sons. The eldest, John, the 'Comely' was the ancestor of the branch who settled in Donegal where their patron was the chieftain of Tirconnell. From this branch came the notable historians Michael and Conary O'Clery two of the writers of the famous Annals of the Four Masters. Conary O'Cleary acted as scribe to the Four Masters. Michael O'Clery, one of the authors of the Annals was a Franciscan monk who spent eighteen years collecting and transcribing ancient documents and Conary spent was also a historian. Daniel O'Clery, the second son, founded the Tirawley branch of the O'Clerys. The third son, Thomas, was the ancestor of the Breifny O'Riely branch of the family which ruled in Cavan. The fourth son, Cormac, was the ancestor of the O'Clerys of Kilkenny.

The clan's former castle of Kilbarron is to be found north of the estuary of the river Erne, 3miles/5km northwest of Ballyshanon, on a steep cliff overhanging the Bay of Donegal. There, Michael O'Clery, chief of the Four Masters helped compile the Annals of the Four Masters setting down the history of Ireland and its leading families. Although The Annals record historical facts in a matter of fact way they are probably the most important single source of Irish history ever compiled and they were written in the monastery of Donegal between the years 1632 and 1636.

A good source for further information on the O'Clearys is an essay by John Healy, *The Four Masters: Irish Essays: Literary and Historical.* In it he quotes Thomas D'Arcy McGee.....

"Broad, blue, and deep, the Bay of Donegal
Spreads north and south and far a-west before
The beetling cliffs sublime, and shattered wall,
Where the O'Clerys' name is heard no more.

Home of a hundred annalists, round thy hearths, alas!
The churlish thistles thrive, and the dull grave-yard grass."

Another O'Cleary historian was Patrick O'Clery who died in 1915. His major work was a History of Ireland to the Coming of Henry II.

DESIRÉE O'CLEARY, FIANCÉE OF NAPOLEON BONAPARTE

In later troublesome times many O'Clearys were forced to leave Ireland to seek their fortunes abroad and in the case of two O'Cleary girls, sisters, their rise to fame was meteoric. Their father, an Irish merchant in Marseilles, became friendly with both Joseph and Napoleon. The men fell in love with the girls but Napoleon, discouraged by his family's opposition to his engagement to Desiree Cleary broke off with her to take up with Josephine de Beauharnais.

Joseph Napoleon Bonaparte, the older brother of Napoleon, eventually married Marie Julie Cleary born 26 December 1771 on 1 August 1794 at Cuges (Bouches-du-Rhone) so she achieved fame as his wife when he became King of Naples, Sicily and King of Spain.and the Spanish West Indies.

Desiree, six years younger than Julie, went on to marry General Bernadotte in 1798 and after his becoming King Charles XIV of Sweden and Charles III John of Norway . She of course became Queen. Her brother Nicholas Joseph Clary was created 1st Comte Clary and married an Anne Jeanne Rouyer.The royal blood of Guaire once again flowed through veins in European palaces. A Hollywood film called "Desiree", 1954,starring Stewart Grainger and Jean Simmons based on the book by Annemarie Selinko, featured these events dramatising her relationship with Napoleon himself.

THE KILLIKELLYS (KILKELLYS)

Other descendants of the seventh century Irish King were the Killikellys whose appellation is derived from Mac Giolla Cheallaigh (son of the follower of St. Cellach). Their traditional territory was in Clanrickarde at the base of Galway Bay with their principal seat at Cloghballymore, north of Kinvara, with land near the modern town of Headford, County Galway. The Kilkellys of the Castle of Cloghballymore, Dromacoo, Ballindereen were buried in the church of Saint Sourney.

Giolla Ceallaigh mac Comhaltan, of the 10th century, is cited as ancestor of the MacGiolla Ceallaigh, Kilkelly family. Giolla Cellaigh, follower of Saint Ceallaigh, was a six-time great-grandson of Guiare Aidhne of the Ui Fiachrach Aidhne. He was a son of Comhaltan mac Maol Culaird related to Seachnasach mac Donnchadh, Scannlan mac Fearghal, Eidhean mac Cleeireach, and Cathal mac Ogan, forebears of the families of O'Shaughnessys, O Scannlans, O Clearys, O hEidhne (Hynes) and O Cathals (Cahills).Apparently the Kilkellys were hereditary olaves (ollamh), physicians or learned supporters, to the O Flahertys.

The Kilkellys held Cinéal nGuaire, the modern Catholic parish of Ballinderreen but their lands were stolen from them during the Cromwellian confiscations in the middle of the 17th century and granted to the Ffrenchs. One of their most illustrious sons was the Most Reverend Peter Killikelly, Bishop of Kilfenora and Kilmacduagh from 1744 to 1783. (See also Killikellys of Bilbao in Coats of Arms). An Irish poet and storyteller Padhraic Mac Giolla Chealla is said to have predicted the arrival of the French in Killala Bay on the day of the Fair of Turloughmore in 1798 to help in the Irish Rebellion of that year.

The Drimcong estate Moycullen County Galway, once held by the Lynch family was sold to Kilkellys in the early 19th century and in 1906, Charles E. Kilkelly still held over a hundred acres of land at there. In the late 20th century Drimcong House was a gourmet restaurant but is now a private residence.There in the barony of Moycullen, James Kilkelly held 5 townlands in the parish together with 2 townlands Derreen and Leenaun in the barony of Ross, Galway at the time of Griffith's Valuation. An estate of over 3,107 acres in the county was owned by Surgeon General Charles Kilkelly of India in the 1870s

Originally the Kilkelly holdings had centred around Cloghballymore Castle in the parish of Killeenavarra, barony of Dunkellin but this estate was seized in the 1640s and the family forcibly transplanted to Raheen and Lydican. In debt, they sold those estates to the O'Hara family in the 1790s. Some members of this very able family practised law and became agents for families such as the Ffrenches who succeeded them at Cloghballymore. Robuck ffrenche lived in Cloghballymore there for a while in the late 17th century.

CLOGHBALLYMORE CASTLE

Originally built as a free standing tower house this old castle has been built upon and extended a number of times by various owners over the course of three centuries. After occupation by the Ffrenchs in the later 17th century it became part of the Lynch estate through the marriage of Marcus Lynch and Surna Ffrench in the mid-18th century. {In relation to both Lynch and Cloghballymore see How Young O'Heyne Slew the Long Black Hand}. Later the property passed down to a branch of the Blake (Ballinafad) family of county Mayo in the 1850s. Llewellyn Blake owned it 1906 but he gave it to a missionary order and was used as a seminary. It is now part of St. Columba's nursing home.

DRUMHARSNA CASTLE

Some half a mile south of Owenbristy is the ruin of Drumharsna Castle, another tower house near Ardrahan is known to have been owned by Shane Ballagh one of the Kilkelly family in 1577 but probably built a few years before then. This tower comprises five storeys, with the ground and second floor vaulted. A spiral staircase, as usual, leads to the top. According to Fahey, who wrote in 1893, Drumharsna was owned by Lord Ashtown of the Trench of Woodlawn. The French family of Galway owned Drumsharsna in 1708 when Roebuck French left the castle to his son, Patrick. thought to be the prodigal of the family, one who nevertheless left no heirs. The fact that Turlogh Heyne and Michael Heyne witnessed Roebuck French's will dated 15 May 1708 together with a tradition that the O'Heynes and the Frenchs were related by marriage suggest that the castle had been another O'Heyne/Kilkelly fortification. After all it is placed well and truly in their territorial area.

Tragically the castle was the scene of horrible acts of torture and killing by the infamous Black and Tans. On Friday, 26 November, 1920, two brothers of the Loughnane family were seized by the Black and Tans, the so-called Auxiliaries together with some R.I.C , while threshing corn on their farm in Shanaglish. A week or so later their blackened bodies were recovered from a bog. Pat Loughnane was a local IRA leader and both he and his brother were members of Sinn Féin. For hours these two young men were brutally beaten in the Gort Bridewell. They were then tied to the tailgate of a lorry, bound together and dragged along the country roads to Drumharsna Castle which was being used as a Black and Tan billet. On the evening of the same day they were dragged to Moy O'Hynes wood and shot. Harry was said to have still been alive in the morning when found but the next day the bodies were taken towards Ardrahan where they were set on fire and hurriedly thrown into a pond which the state salaried terrorists covered in dirty oil. The bodies had been badly burned but whilst they were alive the letters 'I.V.' were cut into the flesh in several places. Harry's right arm, broken across the shoulder was hanging off and two fingers missing. Pat's wrists and legs were broken. Their wake, the custom of keeping vigil over the dead, was held in Patrick Hynes's barn in Kinvara, his house having been burnt to the ground by the British Army. A doctor, examining the bodies, concluded that hand grenades had been put in their mouths and exploded.

Eoin Mac Cormaic wrote an article about the brothers for *The Republican News* in the year 2000 following a remembrance service held for them in the 80th year after their deaths.

Before his death in 1978, Hugh Loughnane, a brother of the murdered men, presented Councillor Patrick Hynes of Loughrea, with a document known as the "The Fate of the Brothers Loughnane: November 1920" written in 1920 by a respected historian, Padhraig Fahy from Kilbeacanty, Gort. With the permission of Patrick Hynes it has been reproduced here, in the Appendix to this book.

THE O'CAHILLS

Another of the leading families in Kilmacduagh able to claim Guaire as ancestor was that of O'Cahill and their influence like that of the O'Cahans, kinsmen too, much have been associated "... with the profits of shore and flood". (See Land of Glorious Adhne) and consequently their coat of arms is an anchor over a spouting whale. They were the navy to the chieftains of Ui Fiachrach Aidhne.

Like their kinsmen, the O'Clearys, they can proudly claim that their name is one of the oldest in Europe. The Irish had surnames from very early times and O'Cahill was one of the first ever. The earliest recorded person of that name was a monk, Flan O'Cahill, who was martyred in 938 A.D.

The Cahills claim their descent from Milesius, King of Galicia in Spain (A lineage which traces to the Gaels of the Russian steppes) through the line of Heber (Eber), his son. Heber became the first Milesian king of Ireland in 1699 B.C., ruling jointly with his brother Heremon (Eremon). Heber died a year later. Eremon ruled for another 14 years. In Irish the name is O'Cathail, i.e. a descendant of Cathal...derived from the Old Irish catu-ualos meaning "powerful in battle." All their kinsfolk as descendants of Guaire can then claim the same prehistoric ancient roots.

In 1000 A.D., the O'Cahills exerted control over much of south Galway, east Clare and western and northern Tipperary.

In early medieval times the most important sept of O'Cahill was that located in County Galway near the Clare border, the head of which was the Chief of Kineala (Aughty), but by the middle of the thirteenth century, their former position as the leading family in Kilmacduagh had been taken over by the O'Shaughnessys and the O'Donoghues allied with the incomers, the Cambro-Normans. In 1222, Giolla Mochoire O'Cathal, Lord of Cinel Aodh, east and west, was slain by O'Shaughnessy. This was the last occasion an O'Cahill ruled as chieftains of Kinelea thereafter the O'Shaughnessys were lords of that district.

During the Nine Years war in Ireland between 1592 and 1601 many barbarous deeds were conducted by the English upon the Irish population whom they regarded as a race of savages. Some it is said were burned before a slow fire while others were racked and tortured to death. It is recorded that an Ambrose Cahill and James O'Reilly, were not only cruelly slaughtered but their bodies were torn into fragments, and scattered by the wind.

In 1653, the castle and lands of Daniel O'Cahill, brother of "Bogh" O'Cahill, chief of the clan in Ballycahill, under the Cromwellian 'Settlement', were 'forfeited' and 'granted' to Edward Annesley under the Cromwellian Settlement. Those O'Cahills moved to Ballyglass, County Mayo. It should be remembered that when historians use words like settlement, forfeited and granted that those words were euphemisms for forcible seizures, lost through theft, robbed during the plantations. Other forfeited property owned by Cahills lay in Tipperary: Daniell O'Cahell's farm in Bollycahell, Limerick and also the farms of Conner Cahill, Ellen Oge Ny Cahill, Ellyn Ny Cahill, Joan Ny Cahill, More Ny Cahill, Philip Cahill, Dermot O'Cahill , Ellen O' Cahill and Mortagh O'Cahill.

In 1757, Dr. Edmond Cahill was parish priest in Kiltartan, right there in Ui Fiachrach Aidhne territory. He was of course a descendant of Guaire, King of Connaught. Mgr. J.Fahey, priest and historian, had a chalice which bore the inscription in Latin: "Pray for the soul of Edmond O'Cahill. Doctor of Theology and Dean of Kilmacduagh, who presented me for the use of Kiltartan Chapel in the year 1757".

In keeping with the subsequent lives of the other descendants of Guaire, many Cahills have contributed to the general good of mankind through their genetic talents. Those people are far too numerous to mention here but living as we do in the age of the internet, enthusiasts can now follow up the names for themselves.

Coats Of Arms and Further History

The official descriptions of the coats of arms of the leading Kilmacduagh families are as follows:

HYNES

Per pale indented or and gules two lions rampant combatant counter changed.

Crest. A dexter arm armed embowed the hand grasping a sword all proper.

Motto: Toujours fort (Always strong)

O'CLEARY (Aidhne)

Or, three nettle leaves vert.

And yet;

O'CLARY'S

According to Fairburn's Crests the O'CLARY'S arms are described exactly as Hynes given above.

O'SHAUGHNESSY

Vert a tower triple towered argent supported by two lions rampant combatant or.

Crest. An arm embowed the hand grasping a spear point downwards all proper.

Motto: Fortis et stabilis (Strong and stable)

KILKELLY

Sometimes as KELLY (There are other branches of Kelly of course)

Vert two lions rampant combatant supporting a tower triple towered or, all between three crescents.

Crest. Out of a ducal coronet or an arm in armour embowed the hand grasping a spear all proper.

O'CAHILL

Argent a whale spouting in the sea proper.

Crest. An anchor erect cable twined around the stock all proper

KEY TO TERMS:

Or (gold); gules (red); rampant (standing upright); combatant (facing-fighting!); counterchanged (here lion red background gold, yellow on left; lion yellow background red on right); dexter (right); armed (in armour); embowed (bent at elbow); all proper (natural colouring); passant (walking); sable (black); vert (green); argent (silver); erect (standing upright).

THE O HYNE CORONATION STONE AT ROVEHEAGH

Irish chieftains were selected on the advice of Clan nobles, lay and ecclesiastical, from among the eligible princes in the 'Dearbhfine', a family group spanning four generations. The candidates had to be free from blemish and of an appropriate age to lead the clan. Once selected the chieftain had to stand barefoot in the imprints of the feet of the first Chieftain cut into the Inauguration Stone. The new chieftain would then lay down his sword and take up a white rod as a symbol of his purity and integrity. Symbolically the people needed no more than a simple rod of coercion to obey the new king. He would not need to rule with a rod of iron! People and clergy would then acclaim him chief and festivities would follow.

The inauguration place of the O'Hyne chieftains was at Roveheagh [Red Beech] where a group of red beech trees once marked the place near the River Kilcolgan runs close to a ruined chapel of Saint Folla, an ancestral holy woman. Unfortunately in the year 1133, Turlogh O' Brien had laid siege to a Hynes fortification near there. He levelled the fort and destroyed the historic red beech tree under which the local kings were crowned as they stood upon the coronation stone. In later centuries the site became known as the Cahir an Earla, Earl of Clanrickards's Chair, situated 200 yards north west from Dunkellin Bridge, one mile south of Clarinbridge on the N18. A small bridge, crosses the River Kilcolgan near a ruined chapel of Saint Folla, a holy woman of the Ui Fiachrach Aidhne.

In the nineteenth century, many people recalled having seen a remarkable stone there bearing the marks of two feet upon which new chieftains stood during their initiation. Regrettably, in more recent times, a farmer had deliberately broken the stone into pieces disposing of them in a nearby ditch. During a visit there by the author, a local woman pointed to a considerable mound near a neighbour's house commenting; "Some old bones and skeletons were discovered there and they were thought to be the remains of an ancient battle. But don' t you tell my neighbour for it would frighten her to her own death."

THE AUTHOR'S SEARCH FOR THE LONG BLACK HAND

It was a fine early evening in May when I drove to the crossroads near Ballindereen [town of the little derry or little oakwood] in search of the Long Black Hand, an imp, which, according to legend, had been slain by a young O'Heyne. I stopped the car on the grass verge and got out to ask a young man who was driving a tractor if I was close to an old church which showed on my map. The boy whose surname, I later discovered, was Halibut (probably Huguenot ancestry as many exiled Huguenots took up residence in the west of Ireland) said he knew of no such place nearby but he could show me the ancient stone altar which I had asked him about.

He led me a few yards across a meadow past grazing cows to a heap of stones surrounded by small bushes. The stones were well cut and probably taken from a ruined church to form an old altar used in penal times. Bushes grew out of and around it. I didn't look for any inscribed stones but the boy promised to clear the brush from it in the future so that people like me could examine the altar so I encouraged him to do so.

When questioned, he said he knew the Long Black Hand! It was a tree? The tree hung over the road I had just driven along. I asked him who had slain the Long Black Hand and he told me it had been young O Heyne who had conquered the spirit. He promised to show me the tree. I said I would call at his home,which was about a mile along the road, after I had looked for the old church, which ,according to my map lay about a quarter of a mile away.

I climbed over the rough, uncut, limestone rocks of a low bawn [a surrounding wall] from a beautiful meadow of cleared land. Within the graveyard lovely fuchsias blossomed in wild profusion. As I walked towards the ancient walls of the church I read some of the names on the gravestones and some of them were modern graves of Hardings & Berminghams, Norse and Anglo Norman derivations!

It became obvious that this place had once been a large site with monastic buildings; probably a seventh century community of monks. The walls were made of worked stones of irregular sizes, very much overgrown with ivy. I entered the spooky roofless nave. It was easy to imagine the Imp, the Long Black Hand, for this was once his haunt, within the dark damp insides. Slabs of inscribed tombstones covered the floor of the room I had entered.

Within one roof-less room at the side of the nave was a huge altar tomb 20 feet square. This tomb looked as if it had recently been sealed around the edges as though occasionally opened to admit more bodies. Iron rings hung on some of its sides There was no sign of an inscribed name. I fancied that Lynch had been buried there or perhaps, "Young Hynes" after he had grown old as the happy husband of the beautiful girl he had married.

Other spaces within the old church were overgrown and musty especially under an archway which led into the nave over marshy, wet grave slabs beneath which lay the bodies of the ancient monks. It was indeed a haunted chapel. I climbed out through a gap in an old window in which a huge slab had been as lowered as a lintel and I was once again in the graveyard where the Long Black Hand had held sway before his defeat by our young hero.

I walked around the outside of the ruins beating a pathway over hummocky ground past the rough hewn stones of the walls covered by hundreds of years of ivy. I came across what may have been a stairway once long ago.

It was the narrowest of passageways between walls so narrow that my shoulders could touch both sides as a climbed the short distance upwards.

The evening was bright and the breeze was gentle and I took pleasure in picturing the life of the monastery over thirteen hundred years ago at the height of its work in glorifying God. As I walked away and clambered over the bawn and back to Miss Cohen's cottage, I looked back, but the old abbey was soon lost to sight as its ivy-covered walls melted into the upper leafy branches of the surrounding trees. Within the graveyard there had been the most wonderful smell of wild flowers. In the woodland returning crows circled to settle down for the evening.

I bid good evening to Miss Cohen who asked jokingly if I had seen the Long Black Hand. I for my part ventured, "It wouldn' t dare touch a Hynes!" She smiled as I made my way up the lane to a place where young Master Halibut was playing with a hurley stick and ball. He took me back along the lane and showed me The Long Black Hand. It was one of the many blackthorn or hawthorn trees which grew quite profusely along the road. Halibut passed many a tree stopping only at this particular one. It was old, and it was hard, and it was thick and it hung like a hand on the field side of the highway and its fingers were those of the Long Black Hand trapped for ever by the virtue of the hero of the ballad.

Later that evening and again early the next day I met Christy Flannery who lived in a thatched cottage near the crossroads at Ballindereen. He quoted easily and readily from the ballad and he told me that an uncle of his who had once been a Dublin detective had written it. His name was Richard Cronnelly and he wrote the ballad in 1840 when he lived in Kilcolgan. The ballad is based upon an older legend telling how young Hynes from Gort in County,Galway, defeated an Imp called The Long Black Hand. Many people living in the region knew the ballad well and one or two recite it for entertainment in the local pubs!

THE BALLAD OF THE LONG BLACK HAND

In olden days when Seamus reigned
And plenty crowned the land.
A spirit was seen in Killeen's church
'Twas called The Long Black Hand.
No traveller ever passed this way
From setting sun 'til dawn,
But was by this malicious elf
Half murdered in the bawn.

The church wherein it lay, was built
By Colman, son of Duagh.
It lay three miles from old Tyrone
And three short miles from Cluagh.

Now Cluagh belonged to Andrew Lynch
A man of large estate
And yet he felt dissatisfied
The church was near his 'state.

Ten thousand pounds would he lay down
And thirty hides of land
To any knight of Irish soil
Who'd slay the Long Black Hand.

And with that too his daughter Kate,
A maid divinely fair,
Whose golden tresses loosely hung
Adown her shoulders bare.

A lovelier maid you could not find
If searched you this Isle o'er
And she was styled, as records tell,
The Rose of Ballymore.

Now this old elf was left at ease
For six long years and more
'Til Lynch's friends a visit paid
To him, in Ballymore.

And annals say there also came
A bold and valiant knight,
Who vowed to God he'd have revenge
On Killeen's churchyard sprite.

Young O'Hyne from Inse Guaire
For so the youth was called,
And annals say he scarcely was
But eighteen summers old.

And yet he would not courage lack
To face the hellish foe,
Who spilled his father's precious blood
And proved his overthrow.

The guests around the table sat
And wine went round and round,
Old   Andrew's health was drunk
And thus he did respond:

"My generous sirs and gallant knight,
Why should I life resign
Whence all of you receive my health,
And drink to me and wine?

I feel like one who cannot live,
I feel that death is near.
For sure will that old churchyard elf
Put end to my career."

The old man then resumed his seat
And tears flowed down his cheek,
They knew the cause of all his grief
But not a soul would speak.

Each man would at the other gaze
But none would raise the strain
'Til young O'Hyne at last arose
And broke the silent strain.

"Now kind sir for me provide
A steed both fleet and strong.
And I'll be off to Killeen's church
To search the ruins 'mong.

And if the Long Black Hand there should be
I'll die or vengeance take
Upon that murdering hellish elf
For my dear father's sake."

His sword he grasped in his right hand
And mounting Lynch's steed
Off to Killeen's church he rode
To win or fail as fate decreed.

And at the abbey gate he stopped.
Where cried he, "Art thou within?"
"I AM AND SOON WITH YOU I'LL BE!"
The Long Black Hand replied.

On hearing such unearthly sounds
His gallant steed took fright.
Her retrogressive pace to stop
He pulled with all his might.

Yet curb nor rein would not avail!
But lo...what made her stay?
The elf had seized her by the tail!
With hellish Long Black Hand!

Our gallant knight well knew the cause
And with one backward stroke
Across the Long Black Hand he cut
When thus the demon spoke.

"ANOTHER CUT MY GALLANT KNIGHT,
IF I SURVIVE YOU'LL RUE IT!"
 "Oh no my friend," the knight replied,
"I think that one will do it!"

He posted off without delay
And soon arrived at home.
He stabled there his dappled grey
Whose sides were white with foam.

In haste he joined the festive throng
In Lynch's genial hall
Where rival wooers were base enough
To pray for his downfall.

So young O'Hyne and Andrew Lynch
Went out to see the grey.
And ordered out two stalwart grooms
To give her oats and hay.

But Palladore did not survive...
Old Andrew Lynch's pride
And some would say that to her tail
The Long Black Hand was tied.

Andrew Lynch addressed the guests
Our hero claimed his bride,
And by MacDuagh's holy curb
The wedding knot was tied.

In peace they lived
In peace they sleep,
'Mong tombs of ample space.
Within lone Killeen's craggy walls
That lonesome haunted place.

This version was compiled from versions given me by Joseph Quinn and John Spelman both of Gort, County Galway. Attributed by Christy Flannery to his uncle Richard Cronnelly, circa 1849. Cronnelly was an ex C.I.D. man from Dublin who retired to live in Galway. He wrote *An Irish Family History*.

NOTES ON THE BALLAD

..."when Seamus reigned" possibly during the reign of King James. The whole line may simply mean "Long ago...

Killeen: In ancient times Killeheyne. The hero's ancestors had given their name to the church, Kil (Church) Heyne (Hynes).

Bawn: a surrounding wall. The old church does have a bawn which in its day must have surrounded a very early monastery possibly built during Saint Colman's lifetime as it is certainly a very ancient church.

Colman, son of Duagh, that is Saint Colman MacDuagh

Tyrone: an 18th. century road map shows that place as the St. George residence while...Cluagh, was, in ancient times, the Killikellys' castle but by the 18th. century in the hands of Lynch. A fact confirmed by the Skinner and Taylor on their 18th. century map already referred to above. The incidents in the ballad must refer to that century.

Rose of Ballymore: Cloaghballymore where she lived of course.

Elf: a malevolent spirit, usually in human form.

There is a very old whitethorn or hawthorn tree which is known as the Long Black Hand a short distance from the old church.

Inse Guaire: In one version this has been given as Inchigore, which is near Dublin rather a long way to the east! Inse Guaire makes sense as it is the abbreviation of Gort Inse Guaire, the town usually just called Gort, where King Guaire, the ancestor of the O Hynes had a palace, a likely place for the hero to have lived.

"Who spilled his father's precious blood..."
There is a true story hidden here somewhere but I haven't discovered it yet! Nevertheless it could be an allusion to His Precious Blood, the Blood of the Saviour. After all the Imp haunted a churchyard?

Palladore possibly "Pall a Dior ", a name associated with the Spanish Wine Merchants, who worked out of the city of Galway. See also the numbers of Irish nobility who went to serve the King of Spain. Galway and Spain have long historical connections.

THE HYNES CHALICE

During penal times chalices, used by hunted priests were often made of pewter. One such is the "Lydiate Chalice", now kept in the Metropolitan Cathedral in Liverpool but another, made in 1760, is the Poulneceann Chalice used by Fathers Edward and Terence Hynes. Their family home lay only yards from a dreadful cavern into which the severed heads of executed priests were thrown. The very name Poulneceann, in Gaelic means "the hole of the heads"; a gruesome reminder of those terrible times. The priests also secretly used a mass rock at Poulneceann for the local population of the Burren after all the official parish churches had been closed. The chalice is now in the possession of the Mrs. Rose Hynes-O'Connor family in Poulneceann itself.

Father Edward Hynes, parish priest at Ballindereen in 1782, was still serving the people of Kilcolgan in 1798. He was buried in front of the high altar in the ruins at Drumacoo. Father Edward was at Ballindereen when Protestant services ceased to be held in the old church on the site of St.Colgan's Monastery. According to tradition the church had become infested with locusts and flies and the Protestant landlord, Christopher St.George asked Father Edward to bless the church in an attempt to get rid of the pests. Father Edward agreed on condition that if he were successful St. George, would accept the Catholic Faith. Christopher St. George became a Catholic!

The Poulneceann Chalice

These two-priestly brothers were signatories on an unfortunate document signed in Ardrahan in 1798. It was a "Declaration of the Clergy of the United Diocese of Kilmacduagh and Kilfenora" against the principles of the United Irishmen and their interpretation of "French-based" ideas. The church hierarchy was making sure that there was to be no socialist Revolution in Ireland if they could help it! A century later the great Irish socialist martyr, James Connolly, would not have been surprised by this condemnation by the eighteenth century hierarchy but he would have taken no notice of it!

The declaration stated: "Should it so happen that any idle clergyman be hereafter found amongst us who, as stranger to the duties of his sacred profession, would unblushingly dare to hawk about French politics and annoy every company with seditious language, we call on the gentleman of those dioceses and order and religion to exclude such a clergyman from their society and to hold him in the light of an outcast and apostate."

What a shame that these descendants of the proud O'Heyne, descendants of Guaire the Generous signed such a document!

THE FRENCH CHALICE

Another chalice associated with priests of the Hynes line is the French Chalice, so called because Patrick French, whose father lost estates in Galway to the Cromwellians, gave the original to Fr. Turlough O'Heyne. The present chalice bears two inscriptions, "1703 The Gift of P French Esq. to the Rever'd Father O'Heyne and his Successors in the parish of Kinvara and Duras" and "P French's 5th deset F.Vts. de Pasterot replaced the cup sacrilegiously destroyed 1866 rev. F. Arthur P.P."

THE O'DRENNANS, CLAN LAWYERS

There is a fascinating old caher, stone and earth fort, just off the N18 road about halfway between Clarinbridge and Oranmore it is associated with the mythical Tammin and Beara, sons of Huamore. The coordinates of Caheradrine are given because it is invisible from the road and accessible only through the grounds of a roadside farm: Longitude: 8° 53' 47" West; Latitude: 53° 14' 56" North.

The caher, also called Caherdrineen is associated with Ó Dreaghnean, with variant spellings Drennan, Dreinan, Drinan, Drinnan, and Drynan, family meaning descendants of Draighnean, a byname from a rendering of "draighean" meaning "blackthorn". The name has frequently been presented as Thornton by semi-translation. The O'Drinnans were the traditional Brehon lawyers for the Lords of Aidhne whereas the O'Cahills managed the 'navy'.

The surrounding wall of the fort is built of massive chunks of masonry 8 feet [2.44 metres] high in places and about 7 feet [2.14 metres] thick. The 'circular' fort is itself is 500 feet [152.4 metres] across and its circumference measures 1850 feet [563.88 metres]. A seven-foot wide gateway faces south. From the centre of the garth, mortar built walls radiate out to the encircling walls. There is an intriguing mysterious carved linear anchor or rather anka on one massive block on an outside wall.

A Bibliography Of Sources

Among the many sources consulted, sometimes just a line or two here and there, the following have been most useful:

Byrne, Francis J., Irish Kings and High Kings, Four Courts Press, 2001

Dillon, Miles, Cycles of Kings , Oxford, 1946

Dillon, Miles and Chadwick, Nora, The Celtic Realms, London, 1967

Fahey, Very Rev. J., The History and Antiquities of Kilmacduagh, Dublin, 1893

Gregory, Lady, The Kiltartan History Book , Dublin, 1909

Kelly, R.J., Article in The Royal Society of Antiquarians of Ireland, 1913

Kilallin, Lord and Duignan, Michael V., Shell Guide to Ireland, London. 1962

MacFirbis, D., et alia, The Genealogies, Tribes and Customs of the Hy Fiachrach..., Dublin, 1894

McLysaght, Ed., Irish Families, Their Names, Arms and Origins, Dublin, 1978

Meyer, Kuno, Ancient Irish Poetry, 1911

O'Donovan, J., Notes on Ordnance Survey Letters

O'Grady, Standish, The Story of Ireland, London, 1878

The Annals of The Four Masters

The Book of Connaught

The Ordnance Surveys of Ireland

RECOMMENDED FURTHER READING

The Book of the Burren, Editors: J.W. O' Connell & A. Korff Kiltartan
Country, A Ramblers guide and map, J.W. O'Connell & A. Korff
The Burren by T.D. Robinson
Ordnance Survey Maps of Ireland sheets 124 & 115
The Book of the Burren, Editors:
The Burren Wall by Gordon D'Arcy
The O'Shaughnessys of Munster by John P.M. Feheney
Gort Inse Guaire ed. Marguerite Grey
Kiltartan: Many Leaves One Root by Mary de Lourdes Fahy
J.P. Hynes, The O'Shaughnessys

SHORT BOOKLETS

J.P. Hynes, A Short Guide to Kilmacduagh
J.P. Hynes, Dunguaire Castle
J.P. Hynes, Fiddaun Castle

Appendix

The Fate of The Brothers Loughnane November 1920

Written by Padhraig Fahy 1920

Amongst the long list of Galway victims there are no names which arouse such passionate sympathy as those of Pat and Harry Loughnane. These feelings are the outcome of their blameless lives and terrible deaths. Of gigantic stature, able, pure-souled, lovable and intensely patriotic the brothers lived a model life on a model farm with their widowed mother at Shanaglish, near Gort. They had another brother away in England, two sisters, national teachers in North Galway, and a brother and sister in U.S.A.

In every phase of human activity in the district, Pat took a prominent part, and was known and esteemed throughout South Galway and Clare. President of the Sinn Fein Club, a fearless soldier of the I.R.A., Beagh, G.A.A. full back, he deeply regretted he took no part in the 1916 struggle, being then a member of the U.I.L. "It grieves me to think that we stood by whilst others suffered, but if I had only got the least inkling of the Rising, and what Sinn Fein stood for, I too, would do my part", he often declared to the writer. He was a well know figure in G.A.A. circles, and shone out prominently in the seven-a-side contests. He invariably played full back, where he was a tower of strength and was the one hurler in all Galway that the giant hurler, Gibbons, of Ballinderreen could not tackle.

Harry was the Beagh goalkeeper and Secretary of the local Sinn Fein Club. Although he stood six foot two and a half inches in height, yet beside his brother Pat he was but a mere stripling. He was not yet twenty two years, and was of a gently, retiring disposition. His ambition was to be a teacher, but, his health breaking down, he rejoined his brother at farming. He was very religious; he helped his mother in the kitchen after the day's toil, and his leisure hours were spent in reading and in playing with children.

On the 26th November 1920, (Friday) whilst the brothers were engaged in the peaceful occupation of threshing corn, a force of Auxiliaries and some R.I.C. surrounded the haggard and placed the brothers under arrest. They

were subjected to gross maltreatment on their way to Gort. There, the
R.I.C. surrendered them up to the Auxiliaries, who, after commandeering
eleven yards of rope at Mr. Coen's store bore them away. On the Monday
night following, a fore of Auxiliaries called at Mrs. Loughnane's and said
that her sons had escaped from Drimharsna Castle, Ardrahan, where a
body of Auxiliaries were quartered. Their friends became anxious for their
safety, and their sister, Nora, made a diligent but fruitless search, calling on
military officers in Galway and else-where, but she feared the worst. One
told her that eight of the prisoners including her brothers had escaped,
that one was re-arrested and that the other seven were supposed to be
"running south". In the meantime disquieting rumours were circulated
to the effect that the Auxiliaries returned to Mr. Coen's with the rope,
that a girl overheard the Auxiliaries conversing with an R.I.C. man, and
that the latter asked what they did with the two prisoners, and the reply
was, "oh, we have killed them" that the brothers were made carry large
stones and run before the lorries, the Crown Forces prodding them with
bayonets, until they fell exhausted, that they were then tied to the lorries
and dragged along the road, that four shots were fired in Moy O'Hynes's
wood, near Kinvara on Friday night, that men answering their description
were seen in O'Hynes's wood dead or in a dying state on Saturday, that
several saw Crown Forces in the wood on Saturday night, that shots were
heard and that the two men were taken in a lorry, and that a fire was seen
near Drimharsna, and that the Loughnanes were burnt to cinders.

Then contradictory rumours were widely and persistently circulated to the
effect that the brothers were safe and well, and were actually seen chipping
wood in Earl's Island Camp, Galway.

These rumours disconcerted the search parties and although one man
found brain matter in Moy O'Hynes' wood when the men who were
supposed to know all about the torture and murder of the Loughnanes
were interviewed, they denied that they ever knew, heard, or told anybody
anything about them. Further searches seemed useless.

The discovery of the bodies came about in a remarkable manner. A
comrade of the Loughnanes often saw Pat in a vision. One night as he sat
inside a stone crusher van, with his employer, "Why didn't you stay longer
with Pat Loughnane?" the boy asked, and when his employer asked him if

he was dreaming, "No," replied the boy, "I surely saw Pat Loughnane with you, and he leaning over his bicycle."

The boy could bear the suspense no longer. He returned to his home near Shanaglish on Saturday evening, the ninth day after the disappearance of his friends. He visited Shanaglish Church and prayed to the Sacred Heart to show him where the Loughnanes were, and that night he dreamt he saw his beloved comrades in a pond at Dombriste near Drimharsna. After hearing Mass at Gort on Sunday, the boy took a comrade with him, cycled to Dombriste, crossed a field to the pond, and there lay the brothers exactly as he saw them in the dream.

The boys told nobody of their discovery until they reached Kinvara. The Kinvara Volunteers, I.R.A. immediately procured a horse and van and went with all haste to Dombriste. They were "men on the run" and on reaching the pond they rushed into the water, and taking the charred remains laid them side by side on the grass. The bodies were hideously mutilated. They were naked, not a particle of clothing remained, save one of Harry's boots. His once graceful figure was a mass of unsightly scars and gashes; two of his figures were lopped off; his right arm was broken at the shoulder, being almost completely severed from the body; whilst of the face nothing remained save the chin and lips, and the skull was entirely blown away. The remains were badly charred. Patrick's body was not charred to the same extent as his brother's. His back and shoulders remained intact. The limbs of both were charred to such an extent that the bones were exposed, the flesh and sinews being completely burned away. Mock decorations in the form of diamonds were cut along Pat's ribs and chest. Both his wrists were broken and also his right arm above the elbow. Patrick's face was completely lashed away, so as to be unrecognisable, and his skull was very much fractured.

Not withstanding that they had been ten days dead, the bodies were in a wonderful state of preservation, without a sign of decomposition. After being taken out of the water blood began to flow copiously from a wound in Harry's side. This bleeding was again renewed when the bodies were laid in Hynes's barn, leaving a brilliant red stain on the linens.

Hundreds dipped their handkerchiefs in the martyr's blood, which they treasured highly. Having recovered the bodies the next problem was to get them away. The Auxiliary stronghold at Drimharsna was only a mile distant overlooking the pond, and the Volunteers were "wanted men". Already a stranger cycled up and enquired casually where the bodies were being brought to. "To Ballinderreen Chapel," was the reply. The funeral had proceeded but a short distance when a lorry of Auxiliaries drove up and halted near the pond, where the Auxiliaries remained searching for some time. They then proceeded to Kilcolgan, and in the meantime the funeral had turned on towards Kinvara. Not discovering anything in Kilcolgan, the lorry also moved in the direction of Kinvara, but meeting two men on the road the Auxiliaries believed one of them to be a "much wanted man" and brought him back in triumph to Kilcolgan Barracks. By this time the funeral, augmented by large crowds that joined along the route, had reached Kinvara.

Whilst the coffins were being got ready, Mr. Patrick Hynes gave the use of his barn for the wake. It was the only habitation left to him, his house and out offices being already burned down by the Crown Forces. This barn together with the dwelling of the man who had charge of the funeral arrangements, were burnt down by Auxiliaries a few days later.

The brothers, wrapt in linen cloths were laid side by side on the floor. The Rosary was recited in Irish. The blood began to trickle from Harry's wounds, and the responses were interspersed with the sobs and wails of a grief-stricken people, whose handkerchiefs were dipped in the martyr's blood.

Soon after, Miss Nora Loughnane arrived. She bore the trying ordeal with Spartan heroism. She insisted on seeing the corpses, and when several tried to dissuade her, she replied: "Their souls are in heaven of that I am confident; and they died for Ireland, so it really doesn't matter how their bodies look. They were ready to make this sacrifice for their country's sake, and because I have the same ideas of nationality that they had, I too can bear this ordeal."

For a moment the fearful sight almost unnerved her and she trembled from head to foot, but, by a superhuman effort, she braced herself together and again she was calm and resigned. "Oh, poor Harry," she exclaimed, as she beheld the mutilated features of her younger brother. She could not identify the elder brother, except for his broad shoulders and his stature. A medical officer was also in attendance, and a number of I.R.A. officers held an investigation and ordered the verdict to be written on the breast-plates of the coffins. When a Clergyman arrived the Rosary was again recited, and the bodies were placed in coffins and taken to Kinvara Church. The coffins were draped in Sinn Fein flags with the letters, I.R.A., and the breast-plates bore these inscriptions:

Padraic O Locnain

A gabad, a marbuigead, a doigead leis na Sasanacaib. Mi Samna 1920 in aois a naoi mbliadain is fice. Dia le n-a n-anam.

Nanraoi O Locnain

A gabad, a marbuigead, a doigead leis na Sasanacaib. Mi Samna 1920 in aois da bliadain is fice. Dia le n-a n-anam.

The I.R.A. kept guard during the night. A Requiem Mass was said on Monday, after which the cortege started from Shanaglish Churchyard, the family burying ground; the members of the I.R.A. marching in front of the procession.

Like their sisters, their mother bore up remarkably well. A British Government inquiry was held on the remains on Tuesday. The Beagh P.P., Revd. Fr. Nagle, repeatedly asked the military and Police Officers to look at those bodies, and say if such an atrocity could be perpetrated in a civilised country. He had been Chaplain to the British forces during the Boer War, and had witnessed many unspeakable crimes, but never, he declared, could he even imagine such a hideous barbarity. Then turning to the younger brother, and recognising his lips and chin, he wept bitterly, crying out, "And oh! Poor Harry too – a saint of God." Ere six months had passed, this good, upright and loving pastor was resting beside the friends whom he loved dearer than life.

Inured as the Galway people were to sights of woe, and steeled by ruthless repression, yet in this case grief prevailed, and there was scarcely an individual in that huge cortege who was not overwhelmed with sorrow. The people had heard of Mrs. Quinn, shot down while nursing her baby by the wayside; of Joe Howley shot in the back at the Broadstone; of Fr. Griffin lured out and murdered on a lonely moor, and a long list of others too numerous to mention, yet they looked on in blank amazement. But this classic of atrocity was too much for them to bear. Strong men sobbed aloud, and women wailed piteously, and there was scarcely one dry eye when the heroic brothers, gentle-souled, noble-hearted and lovable, were laid side by side in a laurel-garlanded grave with the Sinn Fein flag they loved so well wrapt round their coffins.

Pure-souled and gentle, true to God and Ireland, they loved their country and served her well. For her they suffered unparalleled torture, for her their bones were broken, their flesh torn to shreds and their bodies given to the flames.

And this was the fate of the Loughnane brothers, but they were true sons of Ireland, and they bore it all for their dear Motherland.

Ar deis De go raibh siad.

Padhraig Fahy

Made in the USA
Lexington, KY
28 November 2018